superfood
weeknight
meals

HEALTHY, DELICIOUS DINNERS
Ready in 30 Minutes or Less

AVOCADO ∗ LENTILS ∗
SWEET POTATOES ∗
QUINOA ∗ ALMONDS ∗
EGGS ∗ SPINACH ∗ CITRUS
FRUIT ∗ OLIVE OIL ∗
CAULIFLOWER

Kelly Pfeiffer

FAIR WINDS

Quarto is the authority on a wide range of topics.

Quarto educates, entertains and enriches the lives of our readers—enthusiasts and lovers of hands-on living.

www.QuartoKnows.com

First published in the United States of America in 2017 by
Fair Winds Press, an imprint of
Quarto Publishing Group USA Inc.
100 Cummings Center
Suite 406-L
Beverly, Massachusetts 01915-6101
Telephone: (978) 282-9590
Fax: (978) 283-2742
QuartoKnows.com
Visit our blogs at QuartoKnows.com

20 19 18 17 21   1 2 3 4 5

ISBN: 978-1-59233-723-1

Digital edition published in 2017
eISBN: 978-1-63159-168-6

Library of Congress Cataloging-in-Publication Data
Names: Pfeiffer, Kelly, author.
Title: Superfood weeknight meals : healthy, delicious dinners ready in 30
   minutes or less / Kelly Pfeiffer.
Description: Beverly, Massachusetts : Quarto Publishing Group USA, Inc.,
   2017. | Includes index.
Identifiers: LCCN 2016023362| ISBN 9781592337231 | ISBN 9781631591686 (eISBN)
Subjects: LCSH: Quick and easy cooking. | Dinners and dining. | LCGFT:
   Cookbooks.
Classification: LCC TX833.5 .P49 2017 | DDC 641.5/12—dc23
LC record available at https://lccn.loc.gov/2016023362

Design and Layout: Rita Sowins / Sowins Design
Photography: Kelly Pfeiffer

Printed in China

To my daughter, lovingly referred to as Babycakes. So beyond thrilled to be your mom, your cook, and your friend.

Contents

1

Transform Your Weeknights

*D*oes this sound familiar? It's 6 o'clock in the evening and you just got home from a long day at work. You feel pulled in a thousand directions and mentally exhausted. You've dropped one kiddo off at soccer practice and are about to help another with math homework. The last thing on your mind is putting together an elaborate—and healthy—meal. Heck, you count it as a win if you all just get fed—and bonus points if there's a vegetable included. I get it. Life is super busy, especially during the week! And providing a healthy dinner seems daunting, if not impossible.

That's where this book comes in. What this cookbook shows you is how you can—without much effort—provide nourishing foods—superfoods—at *every* weeknight meal. Not weird, obscure foods, but everyday superfoods you already know and love. Each recipe here calls for simple ingredients that you can pronounce and find at all major grocery stores and takes 30 minutes or less to cook. The only prep required is making a single batch of Quinoa-Lentil Blend (page 18) at the beginning of each week.

The recipes are built around the following ten superfoods. Each recipe is labeled so you know which superfoods are used and can quickly decide what to cook based on what's in your refrigerator or what you're in the mood for. We'll explore each of these superfoods in greater detail (see pages 13 to 17):

1. Avocado
2. Cauliflower
3. Citrus fruit
4. Almonds
5. Quinoa
6. Olive oil
7. Eggs
8. Lentils
9. Sweet potatoes
10. Spinach

Whether you're adding spinach into pesto for pizza, lentils into a broccoli Cheddar soup, or sweet potato noodles into pad thai, every dish can easily include a powerful nutritional boost and still taste absolutely delicious.

Say goodbye to the days of throwing a frozen premade lasagna or pizza into the oven or micro-waving a can of chili. Once you start cooking from this book, there'll be no turning back! Why? Because your family will love these quick, easy, and healthy weeknights meals, and you'll love that they're devouring them.

When I started cooking this way, the biggest surprise for me was seeing how much my family loved eating healthy, nutritious foods—if I just *made* them. Why hadn't I done this sooner?! Since writing this book, my 5-year-old daughter has declared cauliflower as her favorite vegetable, begged me to send spinach salad to school in her lunchbox, and repeatedly asks for Broccoli Cheddar Soup (page 52) on the menu every week. And my white rice–loving husband has discovered that, when cooked well, quinoa and lentils are actually good!

What's in Store

As you'll see, almost half of the recipes in this book are meatless. The rest are separated into chapters like chicken, beef, seafood, and breakfast for dinner. Choosing two to three meatless meals per week is not only good for our planet, but also good for our bodies and our wallets (*meat is expensive!*). "But my family LOVES meat and my husband rolls his eyes any time he sees a meal without it," you say? The meatless meals I've included in this book are hearty, full of plant-based protein and fiber to keep you full and satisfied, and, beyond that, they taste amazing. Even the meat lovers in your family will love these meatless options. All recipes have been tested, devoured, and approved by my wonderfully picky meat-loving husband and others around the country. So, if you have someone similar living in your household, fear not!

I flirted with the idea of having an entire chapter dedicated to Sunday prep tasks that would set you up for success throughout the week—things like cooking quinoa, roasting vegetables, baking sweet potatoes, and so on. But, as I spoke with other busy people, I found they didn't want to do a lot of work on the weekends, either. So, the only prep work required in this book is cooking a batch of quinoa and lentils one day a week so when a recipe calls for 1 cup (192 g) Quinoa-Lentil Blend (page 18) you'll be ready. Sound fair?

As a bonus, per reader requests, there's a small section at the end with nourishing superfood-packed desserts like Chocolate-Avocado Bark with Orange Zest and Almonds (page 163), Peach Cobbler with Quinoa (page 179), and Sweet Potato Brownies (page 171).

Kelly

The 10 Superfoods

The ten everyday superfoods were chosen not only for their positive health benefits, but also their extreme versatility, year-round accessibility, relative affordability, and overall appeal. Most you've probably tried before, though you may have not used them in such creative ways! In some recipes, they feature as the main star, such as cauliflower in the Sriracha-Lime-Cauli Tacos (page 85), while in others, they play a supporting role, such as cauliflower in the Loaded Taco Salad with Avocado-Catalina Dressing (page 98). Regardless, you get a nutritional boost in an absolutely easy and delicious way your entire family will love!

2 CAULIFLOWER

This cruciferous, nonstarchy vegetable sometimes gets overlooked when it comes to healthy eating because of its pale color—but don't let that fool you. Cauliflower is full of vitamin C, omega-3 fatty acids, potassium, and vitamins B and K. It's also low in calories, but super filling because of its high fiber content. You can eat it raw or cooked and its mild taste is incredibly versatile, as in the Orange Dream Milkshake (page 155) or the Slow Cooker Pineapple-Chicken Tacos (page 31).

1 AVOCADO

Technically a fruit, not a vegetable, because of the large pit found at its center, avocados are full of healthy fats (alpha-linolenic and oleic acids), as well as fiber, vitamin K, folate, potassium (more than a banana!), and other vitamins and minerals. It also has unique phytonutrients not found in other foods, such as beta-sitosterol, campesterol, and stigmasterol, that are related to its high fat content and that may help prevent disease and keep your body in good working condition.

Don't let the fat scare you, though! We need healthy fats in our diet for optimum brain function, vision, and heart health. Avocados have a silky soft texture when ripe and should be stored at room temperature on the counter (but if you use a portion of an avocado, refrigerate the remainder wrapped in plastic wrap).

3 CITRUS FRUIT

The most popular citrus fruits include oranges, lemons, and limes. They are brightly colored because of their rich flavonoids and are packed to the brim with dietary fiber, vitamin C (which enhances iron absorption, such as with spinach), and other antioxidants. They are great for your skin and immune system. You can use all parts of the fruit—the outer peel can be zested, the inside fruit can be eaten whole (for the most fiber), and the juice can be used in a variety of ways. And, unlike many other more delicate fruits, citrus fruit is very hardy and will stay fresh in your refrigerator for over 1 month.

4 ALMONDS

I could go on for days about how awesome this little nut (technically, seed) is—packed with plant-based protein, completely satisfying, and good at stabilizing blood sugar throughout the day . . . what could be better? Almonds are also full of anti-oxidants, healthy fats, manganese, and more. They help prevent heart disease, assist in weight management, help lower cholesterol, improve brain function, aid in a good night's sleep, make your skin glow, strengthen your hair, and even help reduce stress. Almonds are one of the cheaper nuts, compared to pistachios or hazelnuts, but the price can still add up quickly. I suggest buying in bulk so the price per ounce (28 g) is the most reasonable. The smaller the bag you buy and the smaller the almond is chopped, the more expensive it is! Almonds are super versatile and are sold in a variety of forms: whole, sliced, made into flour, puréed and strained into almond milk, and even as oil. I use some of each form in the recipes in this book.

✸ ALL ABOUT ALMONDS

Almonds are a hugely versatile ingredient and come in so many forms, including milk, butter, and flour, all of which I enjoy using in recipes. Here's a little more about each form, in case you're new to using them!

Almond Milk
Look for almond milk that doesn't contain car-rageenan. It is a common food additive used as a thickener, but its safety for human consumption is debatable. I prefer to use brands that do not use this additive. Additionally, look for unsweetened almond milk, as my recipes add any necessary sweetness separately.

Almond Butter
Almond butter is similar to peanut butter, but is made from puréed almonds. Look for an almond butter that does not have added sugar. Additionally, a lot of almond butters are really coarse and gritty. It's a matter of personal taste, but I prefer the creamiest version available. You can see the difference between two almond butters in the photo on the right. The top one is blended so much finer and results in a creamier texture.

Almond Flour
I love cooking with almond flour (also called almond meal) because it is naturally gluten free and has more protein than regular flour. Please note, especially if you've never used almond flour before, that alternative flours, such as almond flour and coconut flour, can be a bit finicky to bake with. Follow the recipe instructions exactly!

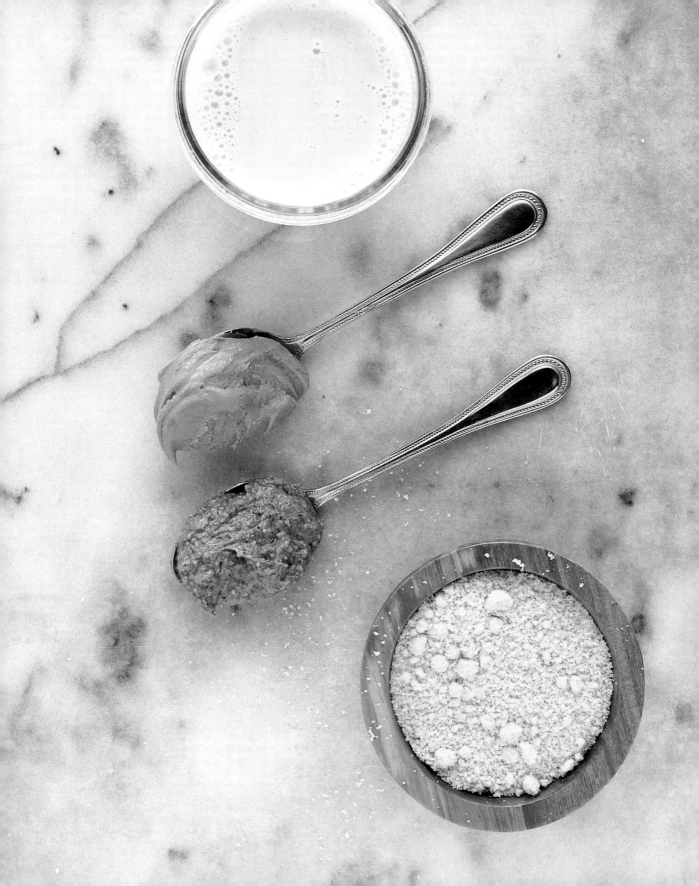

5 QUINOA

Pronounced keen-wah, this tiny seed contains all nine essential amino acids and is one of the most protein-rich foods you can eat. It is considered a seed, not a true grain, and is entirely gluten free. It's also full of iron, manganese, lysine, and riboflavin (vitamin B12), which help with blood sugar control, weight management, brain function, and more. You can buy quinoa in a variety of colors—white, red, or tri-color. I buy red quinoa most often, but, honestly, choose whatever color is on sale, as it can be pricey. The good news is quinoa multiplies once it is cooked, so 1 cup (173 g) of dry quinoa becomes 4 cups (740 g) cooked. I prefer to cook it in a rice cooker (see page 18), but you can also cook it on the stovetop—whatever is most convenient for you.

☀ WHY IS IT IMPORTANT TO RINSE QUINOA BEFORE COOKING?

There is a detergent-like bitter coating on each quinoa seed called saponin, which naturally protects the quinoa from birds and insects. If this is not rinsed off before cooking, it not only tastes bad but also can cause stomachaches or an even more-severe allergic reaction in particularly sensitive people. Some quinoa brands tout being "pre-washed," which is great, but I still rinse it at least once anyway to make sure the water runs clear.

How to rinse quinoa: Quinoa seeds are so small that, often, a strainer isn't really that helpful unless it's made of really fine mesh. Instead, place 1 cup (173 g) of dry quinoa in a 4-cup (946 ml) measuring bowl, and then fill the bowl and with water. Use a spoon (or your clean hand) to swish it around and then let the quinoa settle a bit. Carefully pour out most of that water. Repeat this process six to seven times until the water finally comes out clear. You may lose a few of the quinoa kernels in the process, but it's worth it in the end.

6 OLIVE OIL

Olive oil is primarily made up of monounsaturated fatty acids and is associated with a decreased risk of heart disease, lower total cholesterol, and regulated blood sugar levels. It is especially great for sautéing spinach and sweet potatoes, but it is also good for baking and as the primary ingredient in many homemade salad dressings, such as Avocado-Catalina dressing (page 98).

Olive oil's flavor is fairly mild and, in most recipes, its presence is completely undetectable because of the small amount used. I prefer to buy and use unfiltered extra-virgin olive oil, as more of the nutrients are kept intact this way.

7 EGGS

Once demonized for their possible link to higher cholesterol and heart disease, eggs are gaining in popularity now that they have been shown to actually help *protect* against heart disease. They are also ultra-satisfying (keeping you feeling fuller longer). Most of the nutritional value is found in the yolk, including B vitamins, such as folic acid and choline, vitamins A and E, iodine, lutein, and protein. As such, some recipes in this book call for the yolk only. For maximum benefit, buy organic, cage-free eggs or get them from a local, reputable source, if possible.

8 LENTILS

Members of the legume family, lentils are a great source of both fiber (over 60 percent of your required daily value in 1 cup [200g] cooked) and plant-based protein (18 grams in 1 cup [200g] cooked), and, therefore, are excellent for hunger control and lowering bad cholesterol. They are also rich in folate, iron, and magnesium.

Lentils have a mild flavor that is very versatile and absorbs other flavors and seasonings well. You can buy red lentils or green lentils; I find green lentils to be firmer and more like a bean, keeping their individual shape after cooking, whereas the red ones are thinner and almost disintegrate when cooked. I like alternating between the two when making the Quinoa-Lentil Blend (page 18).

10 SPINACH

This leafy green veggie is super popular and for good reason. It is packed with vitamin K (over 1000 percent of the daily recommended value—similar to its leafy cousin, kale—which is important for maintaining bone health), manganese, folate, iron, and vitamins A, B, and C. But unlike kale, it is much less bitter, more tender, and integrates more easily into a wide variety of recipes. Cooked spinach and raw spinach provide different nutrients and absorption levels. So include some of both in your weekly meals to get the most nutritional benefits.

Spinach should be stored loosely in an airtight container in the refrigerator where it will stay fresh for a little less than a week. Because of its high water content, a large pile of raw spinach can cook down to about 25 percent of its original size when sautéed. So, if you have a lot leftover about to go bad, I suggest sautéing it for use in the Green Smoothie Pancakes (page 143) or the Almond-Mocha Green Smoothie (page 151) rather than letting it go to waste.

I prefer to buy organic spinach, when possible, as it is one of those vegetables that is often heavily sprayed with pesticides in the growing process.

9 SWEET POTATOES

Boasting almost double the amount of fiber as regular potatoes, sweet potatoes are a true nutritional power-house. The bright orange hue reflects their high beta-carotene and vitamin C content—but that's not all. They're also rich in vitamin D, iron, potassium, calcium, and manganese. Sweet potatoes work well in *any* meal—including desserts!—and are so family friendly that I like to consider them the ambassadors of the vegetable world. Because this book focuses on quick and healthy weeknight meals, I tend to spiralize them or dice them finely so they cook fast.

Spiralizing

If you're new to spiralizing, you'll soon make it a habit. Spiralizing is a means of turning regular fruits and vegetables into thin noodles. You can use a spiralizer, such as the Inspiralizer, or a julienne vegetable peeler to create a similar effect. I love spiralizing because it's a quick, easy way to add more fruits and veggies to any meal. Additionally, it allows certain foods to cook faster, such as sweet potato. Because the surface area is increased, the spiralized food cooks in 10 minutes versus an hour or more to bake a whole sweet potato. Zucchini noodles ("zoodles") are a great alternative to regular spaghetti pasta and are naturally gluten free, low carb, and low calorie. Kids love the spiralized shapes, too. Use your imagination to add color and nutrients to all your meals.

Quinoa-Lentil Blend

This simple preparation has transformed our weeknight meals more than any other and is called for in many recipes in this book. It's super easy to throw in a half cup (96 g) of this protein-packed quinoa-lentil blend to almost any meal—oatmeal, tacos, salad, you name it. Besides protein, quinoa and lentils are loaded with vitamins, minerals, and fiber, and quinoa is naturally gluten-free while lentils are very low in calories.

2 cups (346 g) dry quinoa

¾ cup (144 g) red lentils or green lentils

2 cups (475 ml) organic chicken broth or vegetable broth

2 cups (475 ml) water

Preferred cooking method: In a rice cooker, stir together the quinoa, lentils, chicken broth, and water. Close the lid. Press "cook" and about 20 minutes later, when the machine turns to "warm," you should have a perfectly cooked blend.

Alternate cooking method: In a large saucepan over high heat, stir together the quinoa, lentils, chicken broth, and water. Bring to a boil and then reduce the heat to medium. Partially cover the pan and simmer for 20 minutes.

Refrigerate in an airtight container for up to 1 week.

YIELD: 6 CUPS (1.2 KG)

✴ QUINOA AND LENTILS

Quinoa and lentils and are not only currently popular on menus for their taste, versatility, and great nutritional value, but are also historically and culturally important, too.

Quinoa, an Andean plant, originated in the area surrounding Lake Titicaca in Peru and Bolivia. It was cultivated and used by pre-Columbian civilizations, and evidence exists it was domesticated between 3,000 and 5,000 years B.C.E. The United Nations named 2013 the Year of Quinoa to honor the indigenous peoples of the Andes who have maintained, controlled, protected, and preserved quinoa as a nourishing food for past, present, and future generations. Quinoa is also an important ingredient in today's fight against hunger, as it is extremely adaptable, growing successfully in many types of conditions and climates.

Lentils are the world's oldest crop—perhaps being cultivated as long as 8,500 years ago. In recognition of their importance, the year 2016 was named the International Year of Pulses (lentils, beans, peas, and chickpeas) by the United Nations. The initiative celebrates beans for the outstanding sustainable protein source they are: hardy, nourishing, energy-efficient, and practical—they can also be used to help with crop rotation.

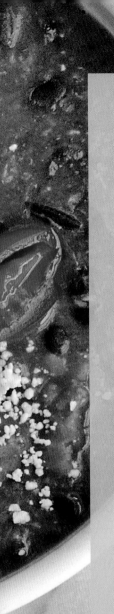

2

Exciting Chicken Entrées

Chicken-Pesto Zoodle Soup

This Italian broth-based soup is hearty, packed full of flavor and protein, and naturally gluten free. I think zoodles make everything better—especially this chicken-pesto soup. You know what zoodles are, right? Zucchini spiralized into thin noodles. Whether you need some comfort food to cure a cold or a warm dinner to feed the family, this recipe will fill the bill.

1½ tablespoons (25 ml) extra-virgin olive oil

1 pound (455 g) boneless skinless chicken breasts, cut into 1-inch (2.5 cm) pieces

1½ teaspoons minced garlic

1½ teaspoons Montreal Chicken Seasoning or other garlic and herb blend

1 zucchini, spiralized (about 2 cups, or 240 g)

⅓ cup (60 g) diced roasted red bell peppers

2 quarts (2 L) organic chicken broth or vegetable broth

1 can (15 ounces, or 425 g) organic cannellini beans, rinsed and drained

1 can (15 ounces, or 425 g) diced tomatoes

½ cup (130 g) Spinach Pesto (page 79)

½ teaspoon dried oregano

½ teaspoon sea salt

¼ teaspoon pepper

Shredded Parmesan cheese, for garnish (optional)

Fresh basil, for garnish (optional)

Parmesan/Provolone Grilled Cheese (optional; see sidebar)

In a large stockpot over medium-high heat, warm the olive oil. Then add the chicken, garlic, and Montreal Chicken Seasoning. Sauté for about 8 minutes until the chicken is cooked through, lightly browned, and no longer pink inside.

Add the zucchini and roasted red bell peppers. Stir in the chicken broth, cannellini beans, tomatoes, Spinach Pesto, oregano, sea salt, and pepper. Reduce the heat to medium and simmer for 20 minutes.

Garnish with the Parmesan cheese and basil (if using). Serve with a grilled cheese sandwich, if desired.

YIELD: 4 SERVINGS

✸ PARMESAN/PROVOLONE GRILLED CHEESE

This gooey, cheesy sandwich makes a simple accompaniment to the Chicken-Pesto Zoodle Soup or a salad for a quick, wholesome meal.

1 teaspoon butter

2 slices of bread

1 slice of provolone cheese

Handful of shredded Parmesan cheese

In a small pan over medium-low heat, melt the butter. Add 1 slice of bread. Top with the provolone and Parmesan cheeses and the remaining slice of bread. Cook for a few minutes per side until nicely golden brown and the cheese melts.

YIELD: 1 SANDWICH

Thai Chicken–Sweet Potato Bisque

Don't know if you love Thai food? This is the perfect place to experiment to find out. The flavors are mild (unless you add a lot of sriracha!), yet flavorful—and you will love how super creamy this soup is! Using four out of ten superfoods means it's a boost of nutrition in a bowl, too.

FOR SOUP:

2 cups (266 g) diced sweet potato, fresh or frozen

1 tablespoon (15 ml) plus 1 teaspoon extra-virgin olive oil

1 boneless skinless chicken breast (8 ounces, or 225 g), diced

2 cups (475 ml) organic chicken broth or vegetable broth

1 can (14.5 ounces, or 410 g) organic cream of chicken soup

1 can (13 ounces, or 385 ml) coconut milk

¼ cup (65 g) almond butter

Juice of 1 lime

1 tablespoon (15 g) red curry paste

1 tablespoon (15 ml) soy sauce

½ teaspoon ground ginger

FOR SERVING:

¼ cup (21 g) shredded unsweetened coconut

¼ cup (28 g) shredded carrots

1 tablespoon (15 g) sriracha (optional)

Sea salt

Pepper

Preheat the oven to 400°F (200°C, or gas mark 6).

TO MAKE THE SOUP: Lay the diced sweet potato on a parchment paper–lined baking sheet in a single layer. Brush with 1 teaspoon of olive oil and bake for 20 minutes.

Meanwhile, in a large skillet over medium-high heat, sauté the chicken in the remaining tablespoon (15 ml) of olive oil for about 6 minutes or until the chicken is lightly browned and cooked through, with no pink showing. Remove from the heat and set aside.

Reduce the heat to medium-low and place a large stockpot on the heat. Add the chicken broth, cream of chicken soup, coconut milk, almond butter, lime juice, red curry paste, soy sauce, and ginger. Bring to a simmer and cook for 20 minutes.

When the sweet potatoes are done roasting, add them to the pot. Use an immersion blender or a full-size blender to purée the soup until smooth.

TO SERVE THE SOUP: Serve the hot soup topped with sautéed chicken, shredded coconut, shredded carrots, and sriracha (if using). Season to taste with sea salt and pepper.

YIELD: 4 SERVINGS

✸ RECIPE TWISTS

For a tasty twist on this soup recipe substitute roasted carrots for the sweet potato. Or add ½ cup (96 g) Quinoa-Lentil Blend (page 18) or brown rice.

White Cheddar BBQ Chicken Pizza

You and your family will love this delicious and more nutritious alternative to a traditional red sauce pizza. The barbecue sauce and white Cheddar cheese give it a really sophisticated flavor.

¼ *cup (48 g) Quinoa-Lentil Blend (page 18)*

⅓ *cup (85 g) barbecue sauce*

1 tablespoon (15 ml) extra-virgin olive oil

1 precooked, premade pizza crust (12 inches, or 30 cm) or 3 pieces of naan

2 cups (225 g) shredded white Cheddar cheese

1½ cups (210 g) shredded rotisserie chicken

½ cup (77 g) fresh organic sweet kernel corn or (105 g) canned or (82 g) frozen and thawed

2 peppadew peppers, thinly sliced

Preheat the oven to 400°F (200°C, or gas mark 6).

In a small bowl, mix the Quinoa-Lentil Blend, barbecue sauce, and olive oil. Spread it evenly over the pizza crust.

Top evenly with the Cheddar cheese. Layer on the chicken, corn, and peppadew peppers.

Bake for 15 minutes or until the cheese is melted and lightly browned.

YIELD: 1 PIZZA, OR 4 SERVINGS

✳ CARAMELIZED ONIONS

My family is not big on onions, but they are the perfect addition to this pizza! Caramelizing them brings out their natural sweetness.

To caramelize an onion, slice 1 onion into thin rounds. Place them in a medium skillet over medium heat with 1 tablespoon (15 ml) of olive oil. Cook for about 20 minutes, stirring frequently until they are softened and browned. You can even add 1 teaspoon of coconut sugar to speed up the caramelization process! These are delicious in many dishes, not just on pizza!

Avocado Caprese Chicken Flatbread

This is a perfect weeknight meal or a great party appetizer! Instead of flatbread, try baking this on 20 French baguette slices.

FOR CAPRESE:

2 cups (360 g) diced grape tomatoes

1½ cups (210 g) shredded rotisserie chicken

8 ounces (225 g) fresh mozzarella cheese, chopped into ½-inch (1 cm) cubes

1 cup (191 g) Quinoa-Lentil Blend (page 18)

1 avocado, pitted and diced

¼ cup (60 ml) extra-virgin olive oil

2 tablespoons (28 ml) white balsamic vinegar

2 tablespoons (20 g) minced garlic

2 tablespoons (30 g) basil paste or 20 fresh basil leaves

1 tablespoon (9 g) coconut sugar

¼ teaspoon sea salt

¼ teaspoon pepper

FOR FLATBREAD:

2 pieces of flatbread

½ cup (40 g) shredded Parmesan cheese

Preheat the oven to 400°F (200°C, or gas mark 6).

TO MAKE THE CAPRESE: In a medium bowl, mix the caprese ingredients thoroughly.

TO ASSEMBLE THE FLATBREAD: Place the 2 pieces of flatbreads on a baking sheet. Divide the caprese mixture between the flatbreads. Top each with ¼ cup (20 g) of Parmesan cheese. Cook for 10 to 12 minutes until the cheese is melted and lightly browned.

YIELD: 2 FLATBREADS, OR 4 SERVINGS

Asian Chicken Salad with Almond Butter Dressing

Shredded carrots, chicken, water chestnuts, almonds, peas, and clementines provide a variety of nutrients, colors, and textures in this salad. Truly a "dinner" salad, it is both hearty and completely nourishing. My husband, though skeptical at first of eating "only salad" for dinner, loves the combination of flavors and eats it regularly—without having to raid the snack cabinet an hour later.

FOR DRESSING:

2 tablespoons (28 ml) toasted sesame oil

2 tablespoons (32 g) almond butter

1 tablespoon (15 ml) rice vinegar

1 tablespoon (20 g) maple syrup

¼ teaspoon ground ginger

⅛ teaspoon sea salt

FOR SALAD:

6 cups (180 g) fresh baby spinach

1 cup (140 g) shredded rotisserie chicken

1 can (10 ounces, or 280 g) water chestnuts, drained and diced

¾ cup (83 g) shredded carrots

¾ cup (69 g) sliced almonds

¾ cup (98 g) frozen organic peas, thawed

2 clementines, quartered

TO MAKE THE ALMOND BUTTER DRESSING: In a small bowl, whisk together the sesame oil, almond butter, rice vinegar, maple syrup, ginger, and sea salt until thoroughly combined. Set aside.

TO MAKE THE SALAD: In a large salad bowl, toss together the spinach, chicken, water chestnuts, carrots, almonds, peas, and clementines.

Divide the salad among 4 plates and top each with some of the Almond Butter Dressing.

YIELD: 4 SERVINGS

Slow Cooker Pineapple-Chicken Tacos

I don't love a lot of slow cooker meals because the traditional cook time of 3 to 4 hours always seems really inconvenient. This one cooks for a full 8 hours so you can prepare it in the morning before work and then enjoy it for dinner! And it makes delicious leftovers, too!

FOR CHICKEN:

2 boneless skinless chicken breasts (about 1¼ pounds, or 570 g total)

1 can (20 ounces, or 560 g) pineapple tidbits, undrained

1 cup (128 g) green chile sauce, plus more for garnish

1 cup (100 g) finely diced cauliflower

1 cup (235 ml) organic chicken broth or vegetable broth

2 tablespoons (28 ml) soy sauce

FOR TACOS:

8 small flour tortillas

1 cup (172 g) cooked black beans

½ cup (45 g) diced red cabbage

1 avocado, pitted and sliced

½ cup (115 g) plain Greek yogurt

Fresh cilantro, for garnish

TO MAKE THE PINEAPPLE CHICKEN: In a slow cooker, combine the chicken, pineapple, green chile sauce, cauliflower, chicken broth, and soy sauce. Cover and cook for 6 to 8 hours on low. Remove the chicken and use 2 forks to shred it and then return it to the cooker.

TO MAKE THE TACOS: Fill the tortillas with a scoop of the Pineapple Chicken. Top each with some black beans, red cabbage, avocado, Greek yogurt, green chile sauce, and cilantro.

YIELD: 8 TACOS, OR 4 SERVINGS

✳ CAULIFLOWER IN TACOS?

Cooked cauliflower has a super-mild flavor, so much so that you probably won't even know it's in there! It has a minor role in this dish, but more of a starring role in the Sriracha-Lime-Cauli Tacos (page 85).

Chicken Salad Wraps

The honey and blackberries give this chicken salad a little sweetness, while the almonds provide a nice crunch. This is a light, refreshing dinner, perfect for a summer picnic—outside or inside!

FOR THE CHICKEN SALAD:

1½ cups (210 g) shredded rotisserie chicken

⅔ cup (97 g) diced fresh blackberries

⅔ cup (154 g) plain Greek yogurt

⅓ cup (64 g) Quinoa-Lentil Blend (page 18)

⅓ cup (31 g) sliced almonds

½ of an avocado, pitted and diced

1½ teaspoons raw honey

¼ teaspoon ground cumin

Sea salt

Pepper

FOR WRAPS:

4 large spinach tortilla wraps

1 cup (30 g) fresh baby spinach

TO MAKE THE CHICKEN SALAD: In a large bowl, mix the chicken, blackberries, Greek yogurt, Quinoa-Lentil Blend, almonds, avocado, honey, and cumin. Season to taste with sea salt and pepper.

TO MAKE THE WRAPS: Fill each tortilla wrap with a generous scoop of chicken salad and a handful of spinach. Fold in the sides and roll up the wrap. Cut it in half to serve.

YIELD: 4 WRAPS

Wrap alternative: Serve this chicken salad in a croissant! The buttery flavor and flaky bread is a decadent alternative to the wrap. Experiment with different fruits, too—strawberries or oranges would also be delicious depending on what's in season.

✳ WHAT'S SO GREAT ABOUT RAW HONEY?

Raw honey is a great alternative to refined sugars, actually helping to regulate blood sugar based on its unique combination of fructose and glucose. It has both antibacterial and anti-inflammatory properties and is a great energy booster. The darker, raw, local honey is best, and many believe it may even help reduce seasonal allergies. Store honey at room temperature. It can crystallize if left for too many months, but it is still edible. I find that I use honey often enough that mine never crystallizes.

Just a reminder: It is not recommended to give honey to infants under the age of 1 because of the risk of botulism.

Buffalo Chicken–Stuffed Peppers

Baking peppers brings out their natural sweetness. I prefer to use orange, red, or yellow bell peppers—basically anything but green, as the green bell peppers are picked before they are fully ripened and, consequently, are less sweet to start with.

4 bell peppers, any color (except green in my kitchen!)

2 cups (280 g) shredded rotisserie chicken

½ cup (96 g) Quinoa-Lentil Blend (page 18)

1 cup (115 g) shredded white Cheddar cheese, divided (½ cup [58 g] optional for garnish)

¼ cup (28 g) shredded carrot

¼ cup (33 g) shredded sweet potato

¼ cup (60 ml) Buffalo sauce

1 tablespoon (11 g) dry ranch dressing mix (preferably organic, no MSG)

½ teaspoon sea salt

⅛ teaspoon pepper

1 tablespoon (15 g) ranch dressing (optional)

Preheat the oven to 375°F (190°C, or gas mark 5).

On a microwave-safe plate, microwave the bell peppers for 2 minutes on high. Slice them in half lengthwise and remove the stems and seeds.

In a medium bowl, mix the chicken, Quinoa-Lentil Blend, ½ cup (58 g) of Cheddar cheese, carrot, sweet potato, Buffalo sauce, ranch dressing mix, sea salt, and pepper.

On a parchment paper–lined baking sheet, place the bell pepper halves cut side up in a single layer. Spoon in enough stuffing to fill each pepper half. Top with the remaining ½ cup (58 g) of Cheddar cheese (if using). Bake for 30 minutes.

Serve hot with the ranch dressing (if using).

YIELD: 8 PEPPER HALVES, OR 4 SERVINGS

If you're having trouble keeping your peppers standing upright, slice off a tiny bit from the bottom to make the pepper "flatter" before stuffing it.

✳ GOT MORE TIME?

Microwaving the bell peppers first softens them a bit so they'll cook fully in the 30 minutes allocated in the oven. However, if you have more time before you need dinner ready, you can skip the microwave step. Stuff the peppers raw and put them in the oven to bake for 1 hour instead.

Broccoli-Quinoa-Chicken Casserole

The dish I remember most from my childhood consisted of chicken, broccoli, white rice, and canned soup. My mom made it every week! Well, I've given that classic dish a makeover, substituting nourishing quinoa here for the more traditional white rice and using homemade mayonnaise. It's definitely an improvement in the healthy category, but no less comforting.

Cooking spray

FOR HOMEMADE MAYONNAISE:
4 egg yolks

⅓ cup (80 ml) extra-virgin olive oil

1 tablespoon (10 g) minced garlic

FOR CASSEROLE:
2 cups (382 g) Quinoa-Lentil Blend (page 18)

2 cups (280 g) shredded rotisserie chicken

2 cups (142 g) coarsely chopped fresh broccoli, or frozen and thawed

1 cup (115 g) shredded white Cheddar cheese

1 can (15 ounces, or 425 g) organic cream of chicken soup

¼ cup (10 g) diced fresh basil

Juice of ½ of a lemon

2 tablespoons (14 g) almond flour

1 teaspoon Montreal Chicken Seasoning

⅛ teaspoon sea salt

⅛ teaspoon pepper

FOR TOPPING:
12 butter crackers, crushed

½ cup (58 g) shredded white Cheddar cheese

Preheat the oven to 375°F (190°C, or gas mark 5). Coat a 13 x 9-inch (33 x 23 cm) glass baking dish with nonstick cooking spray and set aside.

TO MAKE THE HOMEMADE MAYONNAISE: In a large bowl, place the egg yolks, olive oil, and garlic. Using an immersion blender, or hand mixer, blend the ingredients for 2 to 3 minutes until a thick opaque mixture forms.

TO MAKE THE CASSEROLE: To the homemade mayonnaise, stir in the Quinoa-Lentil Blend, chicken, broccoli, Cheddar cheese, cream of chicken soup, basil, lemon juice, almond flour, Montreal Chicken Seasoning, sea salt, and pepper until mixed.

Transfer the casserole mixture to the prepared baking dish. Top with the crushed crackers and Cheddar cheese. Bake for 30 minutes. During the last 3 minutes of cooking time, increase the oven to broil. Watch closely until the cheese is lightly browned and bubbly. You don't want it to burn. Serve immediately.

YIELD: 6 SERVINGS

Almond and Quinoa–Encrusted Chicken Nuggets

These chicken nuggets are rolled and baked in a crunchy batter made with almonds and quinoa. You can use either raw quinoa or cooked quinoa, whichever you prefer. The raw quinoa creates an even crunchier texture, but both are delicious!

FOR DIPPING SAUCE:

2 tablespoons (30 g) spicy brown mustard

2 tablespoons (40 g) dark amber maple syrup

1½ teaspoons soy sauce

FOR NUGGETS:

½ cup (73 g) dry roasted almonds

½ cup (56 g) almond flour

2 tablespoons (22 g) uncooked quinoa

2 eggs

¼ cup (60 ml) unsweetened almond milk

1 pound (455 g) chicken breasts, cut into 2-inch (5 cm) chunks

Preheat the oven to 400°F (200°C, or gas mark 6).

TO MAKE THE DIPPING SAUCE: In a small bowl, mix the mustard, maple syrup, and soy sauce. Set aside.

TO MAKE THE NUGGETS: In a food processor, combine the almonds, almond flour, and quinoa. Pulse until granules form. Transfer to a medium bowl and set aside.

In a separate medium bowl, whisk together the eggs and almond milk.

Line a baking sheet with parchment paper.

Dip each chicken chunk into the egg mixture and let any excess drip off. Then, dip it into the almond/quinoa mixture, making sure to coat all sides evenly. Place it on the baking sheet, keeping the chicken in a single layer. Bake for 5 minutes and then flip the chicken and bake for 5 minutes more. Serve hot with the dipping sauce.

YIELD: 6 SERVINGS

✳ SERVING SUGGESTIONS

Serve these with Sweet Potato & Carrot Fries (page 40), on top of the Asian Chicken Salad with Almond Butter Dressing (page 28), or eat them as an afternoon snack or appetizer by themselves!

Sweet Potato & Carrot Fries

These fries are the perfect accompaniment to so many things—the Almond and Quinoa-Encrusted Chicken Nuggets (page 39), Buffalo-Ranch Lentil-Veggie Burgers with Avocado (page 95), Southwestern Hamburgers with Guac (page 116), and the Buffalo-Ranch Sloppy Joes (page 104) to name just a few! And the best news? They're incredibly easy to make (if you have a spiralizer) and everyone loves them.

FOR DIPPING SAUCE:

2 tablespoons (30 g) organic ketchup

2 tablespoons (30 g) plain Greek yogurt

FOR FRIES:

1 teaspoon sea salt

1 teaspoon ground cumin

1 teaspoon cornstarch or arrowroot powder

4 large carrots, peeled and spiralized

1 large sweet potato, peeled and spiralized

2 tablespoons (28 ml) extra-virgin olive oil

Juice of ½ of a lime

Preheat the oven to 400°F (200°C, or gas mark 6).

TO MAKE THE DIPPING SAUCE: In a small bowl mix the ketchup and Greek yogurt. Set aside.

TO MAKE THE FRIES: In a separate small bowl, combine the sea salt, cumin, and cornstarch.

In a large bowl, combine the spiralized carrots and sweet potato. Pour the olive oil over and stir to coat evenly. Sprinkle on the spiced sea salt blend.

On a parchment paper–lined baking sheet, place the veggies as flat as possible. Squeeze the lime juice evenly over the top. Bake for 25 to 30 minutes, flipping halfway through and watching to make sure they don't get too crispy. During the last 5 minutes, remove the crispiest fries to a plate and put the rest back in the oven to finish cooking. Serve hot with the dipping sauce.

YIELD: 3 TO 4 SERVINGS

BBQ Chicken Burgers with Spiralized Apples

I don't usually buy ground chicken because it isn't often organic or very high quality meat. However, you can have ground chicken burgers and know it's with the highest quality meat. Just grind it up in the food processor yourself! It's super simple and a great alternative to a traditional beef burger.

FOR BURGERS:

½ cup (96 g) *Quinoa-Lentil Blend (page 18)*

1½ pounds (680 g) *boneless skinless organic chicken thighs*

2 egg yolks

2 tablespoons (14 g) *almond flour*

¼ cup (38 g) *diced apples*

¼ cup (20 g) *cooked crumbled bacon*

¾ cup (100 g) *diced sweet potato*

1½ tablespoons (12 g) *Montreal Chicken Seasoning*

½ teaspoon sea salt

¼ teaspoon pepper

2 tablespoons (32 g) *barbecue sauce*

1 tablespoon (15 ml) *extra-virgin olive oil*

FOR SERVING:

8 hamburger buns

8 slices of white Cheddar cheese

½ of an onion, caramelized (see page 26)

½ cup (15 g) fresh baby spinach

1 apple, spiralized or shredded

2 tablespoons (32 g) barbecue sauce

TO MAKE THE BURGERS: In a food processor, combine all of chicken burger ingredients, except the olive oil. Pulse until the chicken is finely ground and everything is evenly combined. Form the ground chicken mixture into 8 round, flattened patties.

In a large skillet over medium-high heat, heat the olive oil. Add the chicken patties and sauté for about 5 minutes on the first side and 3 minutes on the other. The chicken should not be pink or have any pink juices running out.

TO SERVE THE BURGERS: Place 1 chicken patty on each hamburger bun bottom. Top with 1 slice of Cheddar cheese, some caramelized onions, spinach, apples, barbecue sauce, and the bun top.

YIELD: 8 BURGERS

✳ NO SPIRALIZER?

If you don't have a spiralizer or julienne peeler, use a regular hand-held grater to create thin pieces of apple to top the burger with—or even just cut super-thin slices to lay flat.

Chicken Parmigiana

I often thought that Chicken Parmigiana was a restaurant-meal only—too difficult to make at home. This couldn't be farther from the truth! This simple recipe has become one of our all-time favorites.

16 ounces (455 g) spaghetti or zucchini noodles

⅔ cup (75 g) almond flour

1 teaspoon dried basil

1 teaspoon dried oregano

1 teaspoon sea salt

2 tablespoons (28 ml) extra-virgin olive oil

1 pound (455 g) organic chicken cutlets

4 slices of provolone cheese

½ cup (50 g) grated Parmesan cheese

1 jar (24 ounces, or 700 g) organic spaghetti sauce, heated

Cook the pasta according to the package directions. Then, drain and set aside.

In a small bowl, combine the almond flour, basil, oregano, and sea salt.

In a large skillet over medium-high heat, heat the olive oil.

Meanwhile, dip each piece of chicken in the spiced almond flour, coating evenly and completely. Put the coated chicken in the hot oil and let it sear and cook on one side for 4 minutes. Then, flip, top with the provolone cheese, and sprinkle on the Parmesan cheese. Cover and cook for 4 minutes more or until the cheese is melted completely.

TO SERVE: Divide the spaghetti into 4 bowls and top with one-quarter of the spaghetti sauce and a piece of Chicken Parmigiana.

YIELD: 4 SERVINGS

✳ **LOW CARB?**

Serve the Chicken Parmigiana over a bowl full of zoodles—zucchini zoodles—if you are trying to eat low carb. Cooking instructions for zoodles can be found on page 72.

Honey-Garlic Chicken & Broccoli

When that craving hits, there's no need to order take-out. This homemade Asian-style dish is ready in less time than delivery and is a lot healthier too!

FOR SAUCE:

½ cup (170 g) raw honey

¼ cup (60 ml) soy sauce

¼ cup (60 ml) toasted sesame oil

2 tablespoons (28 ml) rice vinegar

2 tablespoons (20 g) minced garlic

1 teaspoon ground ginger

*2 tablespoons (16 g) arrowroot
    powder*

FOR CHICKEN:

*2 tablespoons (28 ml) extra-virgin
    olive oil*

*2 chicken breasts (about 8 ounces,
    or 225 g each) pounded to about
    ½ inch (1 cm) thick*

FOR SERVING:

*2 cups (382 g) Quinoa-Lentil
    Blend (page 18), divided*

1 head of steamed broccoli

*1 tablespoon (8 g) toasted sesame
    seeds*

Preheat the oven to 350°F (180°C, or gas mark 4).

In a large glass measuring cup, combine the honey, soy sauce, sesame oil, rice vinegar, garlic, and ginger. Stir until thoroughly mixed and set aside.

In a large oven-safe skillet over medium-high heat, heat the olive oil. Add the chicken and let it sear and cook for 2 minutes. Flip and cook for 2 minutes more. Remove the skillet from the heat. Pour in the sauce. Place the skillet in the oven and bake for 15 minutes. Transfer the cooked chicken to a serving plate and set aside.

Place the skillet back over medium-high heat. Add the arrow-root powder to the sauce remaining in the skillet and stir constantly for 2 minutes until the sauce is thickened.

TO SERVE: Place ½ cup (96 g) Quinoa-Lentil Blend in a bowl. Top it with broccoli, ½ of a chicken breast, a generous portion of the thickened sauce, and a sprinkle of sesame seeds.

YIELD: 4 SERVINGS

Black Bean & Lentil Chicken Chili

This simple meal is like ooey-gooey delicious enchiladas, but in soup form. Combining legumes (such as beans and lentils) with seeds (like quinoa) creates a complete protein that has all of the essential amino acids your body needs. Feel free to substitute shredded chicken for the chicken sausages, if you prefer. Either one adds a nice protein boost and integrates seamlessly with the other ingredients.

FOR CHILI:

1 cup (191 g) Quinoa-Lentil Blend (page 18)

2 chicken sausages (12 ounces, or 340 g), cooked and diced

2 cups (475 ml) organic chicken broth or vegetable broth

1 can (15 ounces, or 425 g) black beans, rinsed and drained

1 can (15 ounces, or 425 g) green chile sauce

2 cups (60 g) fresh baby spinach

2 tablespoons (14 g) almond meal

1 teaspoon ground cumin

Splash of fresh lime juice

FOR TOPPING:

½ cup (90 g) diced roasted red bell peppers

8 grape tomatoes, sliced

1 bunch of fresh cilantro

¼ cup (38 g) queso fresco cheese

½ cup (115 g) plain Greek yogurt

TO MAKE THE CHILI: In a large stockpot over medium heat, combine the Quinoa-Lentil Blend, chicken sausages, chicken broth, black beans, green chile sauce, spinach, almond meal, cumin, and lime juice. Stir and then simmer for 25 minutes.

TO SERVE THE SOUP: Ladle into bowls and top with any or all of the toppings listed.

YIELD: 4 SERVINGS

Spinach & Feta Quinoa Pasta with Chicken Sausage

I know pasta dishes are most often paired with Italian cheeses, such as mozzarella and Parmesan. But, in this dish, I use super-flavorful feta as a tangy contrast to the tomatoes and garlic. Your family will ask for seconds and thirds, it's so good!

8 ounces (225 g) quinoa pasta

1 tablespoon (15 ml) extra-virgin olive oil

4 spinach & feta smoked chicken sausages (12 ounces, or 340 g), sliced thin

4 cups (120 g) fresh baby spinach

1 cup (180 g) diced tomatoes

1 tablespoon (10 g) minced garlic

½ teaspoon sea salt

½ teaspoon onion powder

¼ teaspoon pepper

1 teaspoon coconut sugar

4 ounces (115 g) crumbled feta cheese

Cook the pasta according to the package instructions. Then drain it and set aside.

In a large skillet over medium-high heat, heat the olive oil. Add the chicken sausage and sauté for about 6 minutes, turning halfway through to make sure they are lightly browned on both sides.

Stir in the spinach, tomatoes, garlic, sea salt, onion powder, pepper, and coconut sugar. Continue to cook for 8 minutes more or until heated through.

Serve the chicken sausage and sauce over the pasta and top with the feta cheese.

YIELD: 4 SERVINGS

✳ RECIPE PAIRINGS

When I buy more-unusual ingredients, such as feta cheese for example, I like to have a couple recipes on hand to make that week so none of it goes to waste. Use any leftover feta cheese from this recipe to make my Strawberry-Pesto Melt (page 80) or the Beans & Greens Tacos with Watermelon Salsa (page 86)!

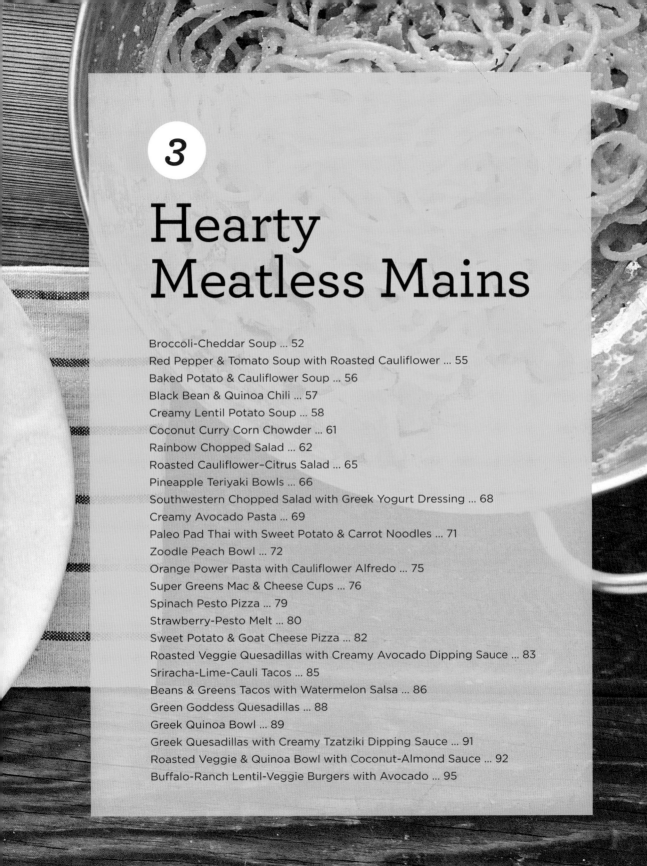

3

Hearty Meatless Mains

Broccoli-Cheddar Soup

Babycakes, my 5-year-old daughter, made the stink face when I first put this green soup in front of her and then negotiated only having to eat five bites. I agreed and then watched her put spoonful after spoonful in her mouth. Finally, she stopped and said, "This is really good, Mommy! Will you help me get the last bites out of the bowl?" It's now one of the most requested dinners at our house.

1 tablespoon (15 ml) extra-virgin olive oil

4 cups (120 g) fresh baby spinach

4 cups (284 g) broccoli, cooked, divided

1 cup (191 g) Quinoa-Lentil Blend (page 18)

1 quart (946 ml) organic chicken broth

¼ cup (28 g) almond meal

1 tablespoon (10 g) minced garlic

1 teaspoon Worcestershire sauce

¼ teaspoon onion powder

½ teaspoon sea salt

2 cups (225 g) shredded mild Cheddar cheese, plus more for garnish (optional)

¼ cup (60 g) plain Greek yogurt

2 tablespoons (28 g) butter

French bread or biscuits, sliced

In a large pan over medium heat, heat the olive oil. Add the spinach and sauté for about 5 minutes or until soft and wilted, but not brown. Transfer to a blender.

To the blender with the spinach, add 2 cups (142 g) of broccoli, the Quinoa-Lentil Blend, chicken broth, almond meal, garlic, Worcestershire sauce, onion powder, and sea salt. Blend until smooth.

Pour the blended mixture into a large stockpot over medium-high heat.

Coarsely chop the remaining 2 cups (142 g) of broccoli and add it to the stockpot. Stir in 2 cups (225 g) of Cheddar cheese, the Greek yogurt, and butter. Heat for 10 minutes or until the cheese has melted completely.

Serve with the bread for dipping and top with more Cheddar cheese (if using).

YIELD: 6 SERVINGS

✳ FROZEN VERSUS FRESH

I like to buy frozen organic broccoli that steams in the microwave directly in the bag. This definitely saves time and gets dinner on the table faster. However, you can steam fresh broccoli the traditional way, if you prefer.

Red Pepper & Tomato Soup with Roasted Cauliflower

This tomato soup is uber creamy and has a lot less sugar than traditional tomato soup made with dairy milk. Forget crushed crackers on top, the roasted cauliflower is the perfect addition—you will wonder why you've never added it before!

1 cup (100 g) coarsely chopped cauliflower

2 tablespoons (28 ml) extra-virgin olive oil, divided

¼ teaspoon pepper, divided

2 cans (15 ounces, or 425 g each) diced tomatoes

2 cups (475 ml) unsweetened almond milk

1 can (6 ounces, or 170 g) tomato paste

¼ cup (45 g) roasted red peppers

2 tablespoons (18 g) coconut sugar

¼ teaspoon sea salt

Preheat the oven to 425°F (220°C, or gas mark 7). On a parchment paper–lined baking sheet, place the cauliflower pieces in a single layer. Brush with 1 tablespoon (15 ml) of olive oil and then sprinkle with ⅛ teaspoon of pepper. Bake for 25 minutes. Remove from the oven and set aside.

In a high-speed blender, combine the tomatoes, almond milk, tomato paste, roasted red peppers, coconut sugar, the remaining tablespoon (15 ml) of olive oil, sea salt, and remaining ⅛ teaspoon of pepper. Blend until smooth. Transfer the soup to a large saucepan. Set the heat to medium-high and warm the soup for about 5 minutes.

Ladle the soup into bowls and top each with one-quarter of the roasted cauliflower.

YIELD: 4 SERVINGS

Baked Potato & Cauliflower Soup

The heavy cream in traditional potato soup is replaced here with creamed cauliflower and chicken broth—but you'd never know the difference if I hadn't told you!

½ of a head of cauliflower, diced (about 3 cups, or 300 g)

2 russet potatoes, diced (about 4 cups, or 440 g)

2 tablespoons (28 ml) extra-virgin olive oil

1½ teaspoons Montreal Chicken Seasoning

1 quart (946 ml) organic chicken broth or vegetable broth (to keep vegetarian)

7 ounces (200 g) plain Greek yogurt

1 tablespoon (7 g) almond meal

1½ teaspoons minced garlic

¼ cup (30 g) shredded Cheddar cheese (optional)

¼ cup (20 g) crumbled cooked bacon (optional)

Preheat the oven to 450°F (230°C, or gas mark 8).

On a parchment paper–lined baking sheet, place the cauliflower and potatoes in a single layer. Brush with the olive oil and then sprinkle the Montreal Chicken Seasoning on top. Bake for 25 minutes. Transfer half of the baked vegetables to a high-speed blender.

To the blender, add the chicken broth, Greek yogurt, almond meal, and garlic. Blend until smooth. Pour the blended mixture into a large stockpot and add the remaining roasted cauliflower and potatoes. Set the heat to medium-high and cook the soup for 5 minutes.

Serve topped with Cheddar cheese and bacon (if using).

YIELD: 4 SERVINGS

Black Bean & Quinoa Chili

This hearty chili is packed with plant-based protein and fiber to keep you full—even without meat. And the addition of refried black beans gives the soup an extra creaminess you will love!

1 quart (946 ml) organic chicken broth or vegetable broth

2 cans (15 ounces, or 425 g each) black beans, rinsed and drained

1 can (15 ounces, or 425 g) organic refried black beans

1 cup (191 g) Quinoa-Lentil Blend (page 18)

½ cup (90 g) diced tomatoes

½ cup (120 ml) orange juice

¼ cup (64 g) green chile sauce

2 tablespoons (15 g) chili powder

1½ teaspoons minced garlic

1 tablespoon (20 g) molasses

1 tablespoon (16 g) barbecue sauce

½ teaspoon ground cumin

⅛ teaspoon dry mustard

In a large stockpot over medium-high heat, combine all the ingredients. Simmer for 25 minutes and serve.

YIELD: 4 SERVINGS

✳ **SERVING SUGGESTION**

Top with cilantro and Greek yogurt! And be sure to bake up a batch of Superfood Cornbread Muffins (page 108); they're the perfect accompaniment to a big bowl of this quinoa chili.

Creamy Lentil Potato Soup

The lemon and white wine give this soup a really light and refreshing taste, while the tahini and sage add big flavor to the lentils and potatoes. Together, you have a quick, satisfying, and delicious meal.

1 potato, peeled and diced into ½-inch (1 cm) cubes

2 cups (60 g) fresh baby spinach

¼ cup (60 ml) white wine

2 tablespoons (28 ml) extra-virgin olive oil

2 tablespoons (28 g) butter

Juice of ½ of a lemon

1 tablespoon (10 g) minced garlic

1 quart (946 ml) organic chicken broth or vegetable broth

1½ cups (355 ml) unsweetened almond milk

1 cup (192 g) dried red lentils

2 tablespoons (30 g) tahini

2 tablespoons (14 g) almond flour

¼ teaspoon dried sage

Sea salt

Pepper

¼ cup (27 g) sliced almonds (optional)

French bread (optional)

In a microwave-safe container, microwave the diced potatoes for 2 minutes on high. Transfer them to a large stockpot over medium-high heat.

Add the spinach, white wine, olive oil, butter, lemon juice, and garlic. Sauté for about 5 minutes until the spinach wilts and the potatoes are lightly browned.

Stir in the chicken broth, almond milk, lentils, tahini, and almond flour. Season to taste with sea salt and pepper. Bring the soup to a simmer and cook for 25 minutes.

Top with sliced almonds and serve hot with French bread, if desired.

YIELD: 4 SERVINGS

Coconut Curry Corn Chowder

The sweetness from the coconut milk, sweet potato, and maple syrup perfectly balance the stronger flavors from the curry and turmeric. You can add some white beans for additional protein and fiber. Or, instead of serving this as a meatless option, throw in a cup (140 g) of shredded chicken. It's delicious both ways!

2 cups (60 g) fresh baby spinach

⅓ cup (44 g) finely diced sweet potato

1 tablespoon (15 ml) extra-virgin olive oil

1 teaspoon minced garlic

2 cans (15 ounces, or 440 ml each) coconut milk

1½ cups (355 ml) organic chicken broth or vegetable broth

1 cup (191 g) Quinoa-Lentil Blend (page 18)

1 cup (154 g) organic sweet corn kernels

Juice of 1 lime

1 tablespoon (20 g) dark amber maple syrup

1 teaspoon curry powder

1 teaspoon sea salt

½ teaspoon ground turmeric

¼ teaspoon pepper

2 tablespoons (2 g) chopped fresh cilantro

2 tablespoons (20 g) raw pepitas

In a large stockpot over medium-high heat, combine the spinach, sweet potato, olive oil, and garlic. Sauté for about 5 minutes or until the sweet potato is softened and the spinach starts to wilt.

Stir in the coconut milk, chicken broth, Quinoa-Lentil Blend, corn, lime juice, maple syrup, curry powder, sea salt, turmeric, and pepper. Bring to a simmer and cook for 25 minutes.

Serve topped with cilantro and pepitas.

YIELD: 3 TO 4 SERVINGS

✳ TRENDING TURMERIC

Turmeric, the vibrant yellow spice, is wildly popular right now—mostly for its potent anti-inflammatory effects. Historically, it was used as a cooking spice, as a medicine, and as a clothing dye. It has a peppery, slightly bitter flavor, so I like to use it in small amounts.

Rainbow Chopped Salad

This salad is a superfood party in a bowl! It's so good, so colorful, and so full of nourishing ingredients. There probably won't be any, but store leftover salad and dressing separately and you've got a nutritious and quick lunch to pack the next day—skip the fast food.

FOR DRESSING:

½ cup (120 ml) unsweetened almond milk

½ of an avocado

2 tablespoons (28 ml) extra-virgin olive oil

2 tablespoons (28 ml) soy sauce

2 tablespoons (40 g) dark amber maple syrup

1 tablespoon (15 ml) apple cider vinegar

FOR SALAD:

6 cups (180 g) fresh baby spinach

2 cups (180 g) diced red cabbage

1 cup (150 g) edamame

1 yellow bell pepper, diced

1 carrot, spiralized or shredded

¾ cup (143 g) Quinoa-Lentil Blend (page 18)

¾ cup (119 g) fresh wild blueberries, or dried

½ cup (46 g) sliced almonds

TO MAKE THE DRESSING: In a large glass measuring cup, combine the almond milk, avocado, olive oil, soy sauce, maple syrup, and cider vinegar. Using an immersion blender, or in a regular blender, purée until smooth. Set aside.

TO MAKE THE SALAD: In a large salad bowl, layer the spinach, red cabbage, edamame, yellow bell pepper, carrot, Quinoa-Lentil Blend, blueberries, and almonds. Pour the dressing over the salad and toss gently to mix.

YIELD: 4 SERVINGS

✳ RECIPE PAIRINGS

When I buy more-unusual ingredients, such as red cabbage for example, I like to have a couple recipes on hand to make that week so none of it goes to waste. Use any leftover cabbage from this recipe to make my Lemon-Bourbon Salmon Tacos (page 134) or Paleo Pad Thai with Sweet Potato & Carrot Noodles (page 71)!

Roasted Cauliflower–Citrus Salad

This salad has a light, citrusy flavor and is overflowing with vitamin C! The roasted cauliflower and dressing combination is to die for! You can even make an extra batch of the cauliflower and dressing and snack on it during a football game or serve as a party appetizer.

FOR DRESSING:

2 tablespoons (28 ml) fresh lemon juice

1 tablespoon (15 ml) clementine juice or orange juice

2 tablespoons (28 ml) rice vinegar

¼ cup (60 ml) extra-virgin olive oil

1 teaspoon grated clementine zest or regular orange zest

1 teaspoon poppy seeds

1 tablespoon (20 g) dark amber maple syrup or raw honey

FOR SALAD:

½ of a head of cauliflower, chopped into ¾-inch (2 cm) pieces

6 cups (180 g) fresh baby spinach

¾ cup (139 g) cooked quinoa

1 carrot, spiralized or shredded

2 tablespoons (18 g) golden raisins

1 clementine, peeled and separated into segments

1 tablespoon (9 g) hemp seeds (optional)

TO MAKE THE DRESSING: In a large glass measuring cup, mix the lemon and clementine juices, rice vinegar, olive oil, clementine zest, poppy seeds, and maple syrup until thoroughly combined. Set aside.

TO MAKE THE ROASTED CAULIFLOWER: Preheat the oven to 425°F (220°C, or gas mark 7). Line a baking sheet with parchment paper and place the cauliflower on it. Brush a thin layer (about 1 tablespoon, or 15 ml) of the dressing onto the cauliflower. Bake for 20 minutes or until lightly browned.

TO ASSEMBLE THE SALAD: In a serving bowl, layer the spinach, quinoa, carrot, golden raisins, clementine, hemp seeds, and roasted cauliflower. Pour the dressing over the salad or serve it on the side.

YIELD: 4 SERVINGS

Pineapple Teriyaki Bowls

Sweet potato noodles are the perfect backdrop for this homemade teriyaki sauce with just a hint of citrus. The yellow bell pepper and pineapple are bursting with vitamin C, and the water chestnuts (actually an aquatic veggie!) and almonds give it the perfect crunch.

FOR SAUCE:

¼ cup (60 ml) soy sauce

¼ cup (60 ml) orange juice

1 tablespoon (15 ml) rice vinegar

2 tablespoons (18 g) coconut sugar

1 tablespoon (10 g) minced garlic

1 tablespoon (20 g) raw honey

1 teaspoon minced fresh ginger

1 teaspoon toasted sesame seeds

FOR BOWLS:

2 tablespoons (28 ml) extra-virgin olive oil

1½ sweet potatoes, peeled and spiralized or julienned

1 cup (30 g) fresh baby spinach

1 cup (155 g) diced pineapple

1 yellow bell pepper, roasted and diced

½ cup (62 g) diced water chestnuts

½ cup (46 g) toasted almond slices

TO MAKE THE TERIYAKI SAUCE: In a large glass measuring cup, whisk together the soy sauce, orange juice, rice vinegar, coconut sugar, garlic, honey, ginger, and sesame seeds. Set aside.

TO MAKE THE BOWLS: In a large deep sauté pan over medium-high heat, heat the olive oil. Add the sweet potatoes and spinach. Sauté for about 10 minutes, stirring frequently to ensure even cooking. The noodles should be softened and not crunchy.

Stir in the pineapple, yellow bell pepper, water chestnuts, almonds, and teriyaki sauce. Sauté for 2 to 3 minutes more until everything is heated through. Serve immediately.

YIELD: 3 TO 4 SERVINGS

Southwestern Chopped Salad with Greek Yogurt Dressing

This salad is like a superfood Mexican fiesta, but without all the heavy ingredients, such as cheese or rice. Light, refreshing, and flavorful, you will want to make it over and over again.

FOR DRESSING:

½ cup (115 g) plain Greek yogurt

⅓ cup (80 ml) extra-virgin olive oil

Juice of 1 lime

1 tablespoon (15 ml) apple cider vinegar

1 tablespoon (20 g) raw honey

1 teaspoon ground cumin

FOR SALAD:

1 red bell pepper, diced

1 sweet potato, peeled and diced

1 cup (154 g) sweet corn kernels

1 tablespoon (15 ml) extra-virgin olive oil

4 cups (120 g) fresh baby spinach

2 cups (180 g) diced green cabbage

1 cup (240 g) canned black beans, rinsed and drained

¼ cup (62 g) diced chipotle peppers in adobo sauce

¼ cup (65 g) salsa

½ cup (32 g) crushed tortilla chips

Handful of fresh cilantro

TO MAKE THE GREEK YOGURT DRESSING: In a large glass measuring cup, whisk the Greek yogurt, olive oil, lime juice, cider vinegar, honey, and cumin until thoroughly combined. Set aside.

TO MAKE THE ROASTED VEGETABLES: Preheat the oven to 425°F (220°C, or gas mark 7). Line a baking sheet with parchment paper. Place the red bell pepper, sweet potato, and corn in a single layer on the sheet. Brush the olive oil on top. Bake for 20 minutes or until lightly browned.

TO ASSEMBLE THE SALAD: In a large bowl, layer the spinach, cabbage, roasted vegetables, black beans, chipotle peppers, and salsa.

Top with the Greek Yogurt Dressing and stir gently to combine. Top individual servings with crushed tortilla chips and cilantro.

YIELD: 4 SERVINGS

Creamy Avocado Pasta

This pasta is, perhaps, the easiest way for me to get my family to eat and enjoy avocados! (Or maybe the Super-Creamy Chocolate Pudding Pops [page 172] are just a smidge easier.) Either way, this pasta—loaded with healthy and filling fats—is a family favorite and couldn't be easier to make!

FOR SAUCE:

2 avocados, halved and pitted

1 cup (235 ml) unsweetened almond milk

2 tablespoons (8 g) nutritional yeast

2 tablespoons (30 g) spicy brown mustard

2 tablespoons (28 ml) extra-virgin olive oil

2 tablespoons (28 ml) soy sauce

2 tablespoons (40 g) raw honey

1 tablespoon (15 g) Thai chili paste

1½ teaspoons minced garlic

FOR PASTA:

16 ounces (455 g) spaghetti or zoodles (zucchini noodles)

1 can (15 ounces, or 425 g) organic sweet kernel corn

6 grape tomatoes, sliced

6 peppadew peppers, sliced

TO MAKE THE SAUCE: Scoop the avocado flesh into a food processor. Add the almond milk, nutritional yeast, mustard, olive oil, soy sauce, honey, Thai chili paste, and garlic. Purée until smooth. Set aside.

TO MAKE THE PASTA: Cook the spaghetti according to the package directions. Drain and return the spaghetti to the pot.

Add the corn, tomatoes, and peppadew peppers. Stir in the avocado sauce and serve.

YIELD: 4 SERVINGS

Paleo Pad Thai with Sweet Potato & Carrot Noodles

This might just be my most favorite meal ever. It's completely grain free and low carb (using spiralized vegetables in place of noodles) and completely over-the-top delish. And that sauce . . . you'll want to lick the bowl when you're done! It's delicious and nutritious. What more do you need when feeding your family?

FOR SAUCE:

½ cup (130 g) almond butter

½ cup (120 ml) coconut milk or cashew milk

3 tablespoons (60 g) raw honey

Juice of ½ of a lime

1 tablespoon (15 ml) toasted sesame oil

1 tablespoon (15 ml) soy sauce or coconut aminos

1 teaspoon rice vinegar

FOR NOODLES:

1 tablespoon (15 ml) toasted sesame oil

1 sweet potato, peeled and spiralized or julienned

2 large carrots, spiralized or julienned

¼ cup (40 g) diced red onion

½ of a red bell pepper, stemmed, seeded, and diced

3 eggs

1 tablespoon (15 ml) coconut milk

½ cup (73 g) sunflower seeds or (70 g) cashews

½ cup (45 g) finely diced red cabbage

¼ cup (4 g) chopped fresh cilantro

TO MAKE THE SAUCE: In a large glass measuring cup, combine the almond butter, coconut milk, honey, lime juice, sesame oil, soy sauce, and rice vinegar. Using an immersion blender, or in a regular blender, purée until smooth. Set aside.

TO MAKE THE NOODLES: In a large sauté pan over medium-high heat, heat the sesame oil. Add the sweet potato, carrots, red onion, and red bell pepper. Sauté for about 12 minutes, stirring frequently until the noodles are soft but not mushy.

Stir in the sauce, stirring to coat the noodles evenly. Remove from the heat and set aside.

In a small bowl, whisk the eggs with the coconut milk. Pour the eggs into a small skillet over medium-low heat and cook for 2 minutes. Flip egg and cook on the other side until the eggs reach your desired doneness. Remove from pan and slice into thin strips.

Top the noodles with the egg, sunflower seeds, red cabbage, and cilantro and enjoy!

YIELD: 6 SERVINGS

✴ SPIRALIZED CARROTS

There's a trick to spiralizing carrots—you have to choose super fat ones. My natural grocery store sells single organic carrots, so I just handpick the fattest ones possible.

Zoodle Peach Bowl

This zucchini noodle bowl tastes like summer with the addition of fresh peaches. While peaches aren't on the superfoods list, they add filling fiber, vitamin A, niacin, potassium, and a good dose of vitamin C. Best of all, you can make this dish year-round using organic frozen peach slices!

FOR ROASTED VEGGIES:

Cooking spray

1 cup (170 g) fresh or (250 g) frozen sliced peaches

1 small golden beet, peeled and sliced

1 teaspoon extra-virgin olive oil

¼ teaspoon sea salt

FOR ZOODLES:

¼ cup (60 ml) extra-virgin olive oil

1 tablespoon (15 ml) balsamic vinegar

2 large zucchini, spiralized (about 8 cups [960 g] zoodles)

4 cups (120 g) fresh baby spinach

FOR SERVING:

½ cup (75 g) crumbled goat cheese, divided

1 avocado, pitted and diced, divided

¼ cup (30 g) chopped walnuts, divided

Sea salt

Pepper

TO MAKE THE ROASTED VEGGIES: Preheat the oven to 425°F (220°C, or gas mark 7). Line a baking sheet with parchment paper or coat with nonstick cooking spray.

Place the peaches and beet slices on the prepared sheet in a single layer. Brush with olive oil and sprinkle with sea salt. Bake for 15 minutes.

TO MAKE THE ZOODLES: While the peaches and beets roast, place a large skillet over medium heat. Heat the olive oil and balsamic vinegar. Add the zucchini noodles and spinach and sauté for about 5 minutes. The zoodles should be soft but not mushy.

TO ASSEMBLE THE ZOODLE BOWLS: Layer 2 cups (240 g) of zoodles and spinach, a scoop of roasted peaches and beets, some goat cheese, avocado, and walnuts. Season to taste with sea salt and pepper and serve hot.

YIELD: 4 SERVINGS

✸ UNSURE ABOUT GOAT CHEESE?

If you are unsure about whether your child (or you) will eat goat cheese, try a milder cheese, such as Havarti, instead. Or, omit the cheese altogether for a dairy-free meal.

Orange Power Pasta with Cauliflower Alfredo

This orange power pasta includes all the orange vegetables: carrots, sweet potatoes, orange bell peppers, and golden beets. It even uses orange cauliflower for the creamy dairy-free Alfredo sauce! Orange veggies are packed with beta-carotene and vitamins A and C—good for your eyes, skin, and heart.

FOR ROASTED VEGGIES:

1 carrot, thinly sliced

1 golden beet, cut into ½-inch (1 cm) cubes

1 orange bell pepper, seeded and cut into ½-inch (1 cm) cubes

½ of a sweet potato, cut into ½-inch (1 cm) cubes

1 tablespoon (15 ml) extra-virgin olive oil

1 teaspoon paprika

¼ teaspoon sea salt

FOR CAULIFLOWER ALFREDO SAUCE:

16 ounces (455 g) spaghetti or your favorite pasta

2 cups (200 g) coarsely chopped orange cauliflower or white cauliflower

1 cup (235 ml) unsweetened almond milk

¼ cup (½ stick, or 55 g) butter

2 tablespoons (28 ml) extra-virgin olive oil

½ cup (56 g) almond flour

½ teaspoon sea salt

¼ teaspoon pepper

TO MAKE THE ROASTED VEGGIES: Preheat the oven to 425°F (220°C, or gas mark 7). On a parchment paper–lined baking sheet, place the carrot, beet, orange bell pepper, and sweet potato in a single layer. Brush with olive oil and then sprinkle with paprika and sea salt. Bake for 25 minutes.

TO MAKE THE CAULIFLOWER ALFREDO SAUCE: Boil the pasta according to the package instructions. Drain and set aside.

Meanwhile, in a large glass measuring cup, combine the cauliflower and almond milk. Microwave for 4 minutes on high. Using an immersion blender, or in a food processor, purée the cauliflower.

In a large skillet over medium-high heat, melt the butter and olive oil. Stir in the almond flour, sea salt, and pepper. Slowly, about one-third at a time, stir in the puréed cauliflower. Cook for about 5 minutes, stirring continually until the sauce is thickened.

In a large serving bowl, toss together the pasta, Cauliflower Alfredo Sauce, and roasted veggies. Serve immediately.

YIELD: 4 SERVINGS

☀ TO BEET OR NOT TO BEET

I love beets. My husband does not. He thinks they're too "earthy," even in small quantities. Feel free to substitute another sweet potato half for the golden beet, if you prefer.

Super Greens Mac & Cheese Cups

These are perfectly portioned little nutrient-packed powerhouses. They have a sophistication that makes them perfect for adults, but also a flavor and presentation that kids love, too. And they make great leftovers, school lunches, or even an afternoon snack!

Cooking spray

8 ounces (225 g) quinoa elbow pasta, cooked

6 cups (180 g) fresh baby spinach

2 tablespoons (20 g) minced garlic

½ cup (120 ml) unsweetened almond milk

¼ cup (60 ml) extra-virgin olive oil

1 cup (40 g) chopped fresh basil leaves

1 can (14 ounces, or 390 g) quartered artichoke hearts, drained and diced

2 tablespoons (14 g) ground flaxseed

1 teaspoon sea salt

½ teaspoon pepper

2 cups (230 g) shredded mozzarella cheese

Preheat the oven to 375°F (190°C, or gas mark 5). Spray a 12-cup muffin tin with nonstick cooking spray and set aside.

In a large skillet over medium heat, sauté the spinach and garlic for 5 minutes. Stir frequently. The spinach should be wilted, but not burned. Remove from the heat and cut the spinach into bite-size pieces. Transfer to a large bowl.

Stir in the almond milk, olive oil, basil, artichoke hearts, flaxseed, sea salt, and pepper. Sprinkle the mozzarella cheese over top and stir again to combine.

Evenly distribute the mac and cheese mixture into the muffin cups. Bake for 25 minutes or until the tops are golden brown.

YIELD: 12 MAC AND CHEESE CUPS, OR 6 SERVINGS

✳ WHAT'S SO GREAT ABOUT FLAX?

Flaxseed is full of omega-3 fatty acids, antioxidants, and fiber. It has a really mild flavor—almost a little nutty. I love adding a tablespoon (7 g) into smoothies, sauces, and other things for the nutrient boost. You can also use flaxseed as an egg substitute; it's very common in vegan baking. To make 1 "flax egg:" Mix 1 tablespoon (7 g) flaxseed with 3 tablespoons (45 ml) warm water and refrigerate for 15 minutes.

Spinach Pesto Pizza

I am absolutely in love with this pesto. It's so creamy and delicious and no one would guess there are 4 cups (120 g) of spinach hiding in there! (Think of the nutritional benefits, too!) And it couldn't be easier to make: Put everything in a food processor and swirl. The peppadew peppers add a nice tang to the pizza, too.

FOR SPINACH PESTO:

¼ cup (60 g) basil paste or 20 fresh basil leaves

4 cups (120 g) fresh baby spinach

½ cup (68 g) pine nuts

½ cup (120 ml) extra-virgin olive oil

⅓ cup (33 g) grated Parmesan cheese

2 tablespoons (14 g) ground flaxseed

1 tablespoon (10 g) minced garlic

1½ teaspoons coconut sugar

1 teaspoon fresh lemon juice

⅛ teaspoon sea salt

⅛ teaspoon ground pepper

FOR PIZZA:

1 precooked, premade pizza crust (12 inches, or 30 cm) or 3 pieces of naan

1 cup (115 g) shredded mozzarella cheese

8 peppadew peppers

8 grape tomatoes, thinly sliced

TO MAKE THE SPINACH PESTO: In a food processor, combine all the Spinach Pesto ingredients and blend until smooth.

TO MAKE THE PIZZA: Preheat the oven to 425°F (220°C, or gas mark 7).

Spread about ⅔ cup (about 175 g) of Spinach Pesto onto the precooked pizza crust so it's about ¼-inch (0.6 cm) thick. Top with the mozzarella cheese, peppadew peppers, and tomatoes. (Of course, you can substitute your favorite toppings, if you prefer.) Bake for 10 minutes or until the cheese is melted and lightly browned.

YIELD: 1 PIZZA, OR 4 SERVINGS, PLUS EXTRA PESTO

✳ WHAT TO DO WITH THE EXTRA PESTO!

This recipe makes more pesto than you need for one pizza. So you can do any of the following with the extra:

- Save it for a future pizza.
- Make the Strawberry-Pesto Melt (page 80).
- Put it in a quesadilla with turkey and cheese.
- Make the Chicken-Pesto Zoodle Soup (page 22).
- Serve it over penne or any other pasta.

Strawberry-Pesto Melt

These sandwiches finished cooking just when my husband walked in the door from work. And, I must confess, I got "the look." You might have a similar spousal look of disapproval in your house. This was a fairly simple meal, but definitely not traditional. But, to my surprise (and his!), he actually uttered that he liked it and the flavors complemented each other well, and that it was good . . . REALLY good. *"What was that, Honey? I couldn't hear you . . . ."*

½ cup (130 g) Spinach Pesto (page 79)

6 fresh organic strawberries, sliced

8 ounces (225 g) fontina cheese, thinly sliced

¼ cup (38 g) crumbled feta cheese

8 slices of bread of choice

Preheat the oven to 375°F (190°C, or gas mark 5). Alternatively, you can use a toaster oven.

TO ASSEMBLE THE SANDWICHES: Spread an even layer of Spinach Pesto onto one side of the bread slices and then top with a single layer of strawberries. Add some fontina cheese and a few sprinkles of feta cheese. Top with the other slice of bread and place the sandwiches on a parchment paper–lined baking sheet. Bake for 10 minutes, flipping halfway through, until the cheese is completely melted and the bread is toasted.

YIELD: 4 SANDWICHES

Some may consider organic fruits a splurge, but I recently discovered that organic strawberries are not only healthier for you, they are so much sweeter, too! That's definitely worth the extra dollar (or two) to me.

✹ MAKE THIS SANDWICH INTO A PIZZA!

Instead of the toppings used on the Spinach Pesto Pizza (page 79)—peppadew peppers and grape tomatoes—try sliced strawberries and feta instead! It's a perfect summertime dinner.

Sweet Potato & Goat Cheese Pizza

The sweetness of the figs and sweet potato complement each other nicely and serve as the perfect juxtaposition to the more strongly flavored goat cheese and walnuts.

½ of a sweet potato, thinly sliced

1 tablespoon (15 ml) extra-virgin olive oil

½ cup (123 g) pizza sauce

1 precooked, premade pizza crust (12 inches, or 30 cm) or 3 pieces of naan

1 cup (115 g) shredded mozzarella cheese

3 dried figs, sliced

½ cup (75 g) crumbled goat cheese

½ cup (60 g) coarsely chopped walnuts

Preheat the oven to 425°F (220°C, or gas mark 7).

On a parchment paper–lined baking sheet, place the sweet potato slices in a single layer. Brush with olive oil. Bake for 15 minutes.

Spoon the pizza sauce over the crust. Top with the mozzarella cheese. Lay the roasted sweet potato slices and fig slices on top. Sprinkle on the goat cheese and walnuts. Return the pizza to the oven and bake for 10 minutes more or until the cheese is melted and lightly browned.

YIELD: 1 PIZZA, OR 4 SERVINGS

✱ RECIPE PAIRINGS

When I buy more unusual ingredients, such as goat cheese, I like to have a couple recipes on hand to make that week so none of it goes to waste. Use any leftover goat cheese from this recipe to make my Zoodle Peach Bowl on page 72 or my Salmon Quesadillas on page 127!

Roasted Veggie Quesadillas with Creamy Avocado Dipping Sauce

I love making quesadillas for dinner because they're hot, melty, stuffed with goodness, super quick to make, and everyone devours them—without complaining or arguing!

FOR ROASTED VEGGIES

½ of a sweet potato, cut in ½-inch (1 cm) chunks

½ cup (50 g) coarsely chopped cauliflower

½ of a bell pepper, any color, cut in ½-inch (1 cm) chunks

½ of a zucchini, cut in ½-inch (1 cm) chunks

4 button mushrooms, coarsely chopped

2 tablespoons (28 ml) extra-virgin olive oil

Juice of ½ of a lemon

1 teaspoon lemon pepper seasoning

FOR DIPPING SAUCE:

1 avocado

¼ cup (60 g) plain Greek yogurt

¼ cup (60 g) tahini

Juice of ½ of a lemon

1 tablespoon (15 ml) balsamic vinegar

FOR QUESADILLAS:

4 large tortillas

1½ cups (175 g) shredded Italian cheese blend

Butter, for cooking

TO MAKE THE ROASTED VEGGIES: Preheat the oven to 425°F (220°C, or gas mark 7). On a parchment paper–lined baking sheet, spread the sweet potato, cauliflower, bell pepper, zucchini, and mushrooms in a single layer. Brush with the olive oil, squeeze on the lemon juice, and sprinkle with the lemon pepper. Bake for 15 minutes.

TO MAKE THE CREAMY AVOCADO DIPPING SAUCE: In a large glass measuring cup, combine the avocado, Greek yogurt, tahini, lemon juice, and balsamic vinegar. Using an immersion blender, or in a food processor, purée the sauce. Set aside.

TO MAKE THE QUESADILLAS: Place 2 tortillas on a work surface. Top each with a large handful of Italian cheese blend and then with the roasted veggies. Cover with the 2 remaining tortillas.

In a large skillet over medium heat, melt some butter. Carefully transfer 1 quesadilla to the skillet (or assemble it directly in the pan after the butter melts). Spread some more butter on top of the quesadilla. Cook for 3 or 4 minutes per side until the tortilla is golden brown and the cheese is melted. Transfer to a plate to keep warm and repeat, cooking the remaining quesadilla. Slice into triangles and serve with Creamy Avocado Dipping sauce.

YIELD: 2 QUESADILLAS, OR 4 SERVINGS

Sriracha-Lime-Cauli Tacos

Tacos aren't just for Tuesdays with this recipe. These tacos are so super easy to make and bursting with flavors so bright and fresh, you can make them any time the mood hits. And, if you like things a little spicier, add more sriracha! Let the kids assemble their own tacos to get everyone involved in the meal.

FOR CAULIFLOWER FILLING:

Cooking spray

4 cups (400 g) coarsely chopped cauliflower

Juice of 1 lime

1 tablespoon (15 ml) extra-virgin olive oil

1 teaspoon chili powder

1 teaspoon sriracha

1 teaspoon minced garlic

½ teaspoon ground cumin

½ teaspoon sea salt

FOR TACOS:

8 small flour tortillas

1 avocado, sliced

½ cup (45 g) thinly sliced red cabbage

½ cup (125 g) Mango Salsa (see sidebar)

1 tablespoon (1 g) chopped fresh cilantro

2 tablespoons (30 g) sriracha

TO MAKE THE CAULIFLOWER FILLING: Preheat the oven to 425°F (220°C, or gas mark 7). Line a baking sheet with parchment paper or spray it with nonstick cooking spray.

In a large bowl, combine the cauliflower, lime juice, olive oil, chili powder, sriracha, garlic, cumin, and sea salt. Stir until the cauliflower pieces are evenly coated with the seasonings. Transfer to the baking sheet in a single layer and bake the cauliflower for 30 minutes.

TO MAKE THE TACOS: Fill each tortilla with a scoop of roasted cauliflower, and then top with avocado, red cabbage, Mango Salsa, and cilantro. Drizzle sriracha over top. Fold and feast!

YIELD: 8 TACOS, OR 4 SERVINGS

✳ MANGO SALSA

If you don't have a favorite purchased variety of mango salsa, make your own! Use the Watermelon Salsa recipe (page 86), but substitute diced mango for the watermelon. This salsa can also dress up chicken or fish, if you like.

Beans & Greens Tacos with Watermelon Salsa

I am absolutely obsessed with tacos and for more than just a few reasons. They're beyond delicious. They're super versatile—you can stuff them with just about anything (veggies, chicken, fish, flank steak—I love all tacos). You can dress them up with various salsas and guacamoles (peach guac, sriracha corn salsa, the super summery watermelon salsa in this recipe, etc.), and everyone loves them! Oh, did I mention they make mealtime fun, too?

FOR TACOS:

2 cups (60 g) fresh baby spinach

1 cup (164 g) frozen organic sweet corn kernels

1 can (15 ounces, or 425 g) black beans, rinsed and drained

½ cup (96 g) Quinoa-Lentil Blend (page 18)

½ cup (60 g) coarsely chopped walnuts

2 tablespoons (32 g) salsa

1 tablespoon (8 g) taco seasoning

1 teaspoon ground cumin

8 small tortillas

½ cup (75 g) crumbled feta cheese

1 avocado (optional)

FOR WATERMELON SALSA:

1 cup (150 g) finely diced watermelon

¼ cup (65 g) salsa

1 tablespoon (1 g) chopped fresh cilantro leaves

¼ teaspoon paprika

⅛ teaspoon sea salt

Preheat the oven to 350°F (180°C, or gas mark 4).

TO MAKE THE TACOS: In a large skillet over medium-high heat, combine the spinach, corn, black beans, Quinoa-Lentil Blend, walnuts, salsa, taco seasoning, and cumin. Sauté for 10 minutes or until heated through and the spinach is wilted.

TO MAKE THE WATERMELON SALSA: Meanwhile, in a small bowl, stir together the watermelon, salsa, cilantro, paprika, and sea salt until thoroughly combined.

TO ASSEMBLE THE TACOS: Place a large spoonful of taco filling on each tortilla, followed by a large dollop of watermelon salsa, a sprinkle of feta cheese, and a few avocado slices (if using).

YIELD: 8 TACOS, OR 4 SERVINGS

✴ FRUIT SALSA

Watermelon is such a light and refreshing fruit and it gives a unique sweetness and summery taste to these tacos. If it is not in season, though, try mango or even canned pineapple or peaches (available year-round). Any sweet fruit will do!

Green Goddess Quesadillas

There's so much green goodness going on in these Green Goddess Quesadillas! Healthy fats from the avocado and pistachios and vitamin K and fiber from the peas and basil combine to create something uber nourishing and delicious!

1½ teaspoons extra-virgin olive oil

4 cups (120 g) fresh baby spinach

½ cup (75 g) green peas, divided

1½ teaspoons minced garlic

Juice of ½ of a lime

1 avocado, mashed

1 tablespoon (15 g) basil paste

4 large tortillas

1½ cups (175 g) shredded
   mozzarella cheese, divided

½ cup (62 g) pistachios, coarsely
   chopped, divided

Butter, for cooking

In a large skillet over medium-high heat, heat the olive oil. Add the spinach, peas, and garlic and sauté for about 5 minutes. The spinach should be wilted, but not blackened. Squeeze the lime juice over the vegetables.

In a small bowl, mash the avocado with a fork and stir in the basil paste.

TO MAKE THE QUESADILLAS: Place 2 tortillas on a work surface. Spread each with half of the avocado mixture in a thin layer. Then sprinkle each with a large handful of mozzarella cheese. Top the cheese with half of the sautéed spinach and peas. Sprinkle ¼ cup (31 g) of pistachios over each quesadilla and then top each with another tortilla.

In a large skillet over medium heat, melt some butter. Carefully transfer 1 quesadilla to the skillet (or assemble it directly in the pan after the butter melts). Spread some more butter on top of the quesadilla. Cook for 3 or 4 minutes per side until the tortilla is golden brown and the cheese is melted. Transfer to a plate to keep warm and repeat, cooking the remaining quesadilla. Slice into triangles and serve hot.

YIELD: 2 QUESADILLAS, OR 4 SERVINGS

Greek Quinoa Bowl

This recipe was inspired by one of my favorite restaurant meals. The flavors and textures are divine. You can eat it as more of a "rice" bowl or serve a big dollop over a bed of greens.

2½ *cups (478 g) Quinoa-Lentil Blend (page 18)*

1 *cup (240 g) Creamy Tzatziki Dipping Sauce (page 91)*

1 *cup (180 g) grape tomatoes, diced*

1 *cup (180 g) roasted red bell peppers, diced*

1 *cup (240 g) chickpeas, rinsed and drained*

1 *cup (150 g) crumbled feta cheese*

½ *cup (50 g) diced black olives*

½ *cup (60 g) diced pepperoncini*

¼ *cup (40 g) diced red onion*

In a large bowl, stir together the Quinoa-Lentil Blend, Creamy Tzatziki Dipping Sauce, tomatoes, roasted red bell peppers, chickpeas, feta cheese, olives, pepperoncini, and red onion. Chill before serving.

YIELD: 4 SERVINGS

> ✳ **MAKE IT A WRAP!**
>
> Combine 1 cup (210 g) of the Greek Quinoa Bowl mixture with a handful of spinach and wrap it up for a quick lunch to go.

Greek Quesadillas with Creamy Tzatziki Dipping Sauce

First, let's talk about this sauce! You will want to dip all things in it. Next, let's talk quesadillas: These are super easy to make, full of flavor, filled with two kinds of cheese, and then dipped in the most amazing tzatziki sauce (did I mention that?)! Be sure to use the finest grater to shred the cucumber.

FOR DIPPING SAUCE:

⅓ cup (77 g) sour cream

⅓ cup (40 g) shredded cucumber

1 tablespoon (15 ml) fresh lemon juice

1 tablespoon (15 ml) extra-virgin olive oil

¼ teaspoon sea salt

⅛ teaspoon pepper

FOR QUESADILLAS:

4 large tortillas

1 cup (115 g) shredded mozzarella cheese

10 grape tomatoes, sliced

½ cup (50 g) sliced black olives

½ cup (90 g) diced roasted red bell pepper

½ cup (96 g) Quinoa-Lentil Blend (page 18)

½ cup (75 g) crumbled feta cheese

Butter, for cooking

TO MAKE THE CREAMY TZATZIKI DIPPING SAUCE: In a small bowl, stir together the sour cream, cucumber, lemon juice, olive oil, sea salt, and pepper. Refrigerate until the quesadillas are done.

TO MAKE THE QUESADILLAS: Place 2 tortillas on a work surface. Spread a large handful of mozzarella cheese on each tortilla. Top each with half of the tomatoes, black olives, roasted red bell pepper, Quinoa-Lentil Blend, and feta cheese. Top each with another tortilla.

In a large skillet over medium heat, melt some butter. Carefully transfer 1 quesadilla to the skillet (or assemble it directly in the pan after the butter melts). Spread some more butter on top of the quesadilla. Cook for 3 or 4 minutes per side until the tortilla is golden brown and the cheese is melted. Transfer to a plate to keep warm and repeat, cooking the remaining quesadilla. Slice into triangles and serve hot with the Creamy Tzatziki Dipping Sauce.

YIELD: 2 QUESADILLAS, OR 4 SERVINGS

Roasted Veggie & Quinoa Bowl with Coconut-Almond Sauce

This is a perfect way to enjoy a variety of vegetables—perfectly roasted and then topped with a creamy, salty, sweet, coconut-y, delicious sauce. You can mix up the kinds of veggies you use depending on what you have in the fridge! I've made this with asparagus, tomatoes, and even grilled chicken before.

FOR SAUCE:

1 cup (240 g) canned chickpeas, rinsed and drained

⅓ cup (80 ml) coconut milk

½ cup (130 g) almond butter

2 tablespoons (40 g) dark amber maple syrup

1 tablespoon (15 ml) soy sauce

1 tablespoon (15 ml) fresh key lime juice or regular lime juice

1 teaspoon minced garlic

FOR VEGGIE BOWL:

Cooking spray

2 red bell peppers, cut into bite-size pieces

2 large carrots, cut into bite-size pieces

1 large sweet potato, peeled and cut into bite-size pieces

6 radishes or 1 beet, cut into bite-size pieces

2 cups (370 g) cooked quinoa, divided

TO MAKE THE COCONUT-ALMOND SAUCE: In a large glass measuring cup, combine the chickpeas and coconut milk. Using an immersion blender, or in a food processor, purée them.

Stir in the almond butter, maple syrup, soy sauce, key lime juice, and garlic until blended and smooth. Set aside.

TO MAKE THE VEGGIE BOWLS: Preheat the oven to 425°F (220°C, or gas mark 7). Line a baking sheet with parchment paper or spray with nonstick cooking spray.

Arrange the red bell peppers, carrots, sweet potato, and radishes in a single layer on the prepared sheet. Bake for 30 minutes or until everything is softened and lightly browned.

TO ASSEMBLE EACH BOWL: Place ½ cup (93 g) of quinoa into each of 4 bowls. Top each with a generous portion of roasted veggies and a large dollop of Coconut-Almond Sauce.

YIELD: 4 SERVINGS

✴ RADISHES

Roasted radishes are a bit "earthy" for my husband and kiddo, but they sure are pretty! Feel free to substitute roasted beets or caramelized onions, if you prefer.

Buffalo-Ranch Lentil-Veggie Burgers with Avocado

These veggie burgers have so much protein, it's crazy (15 grams per burger, to be exact)! They have a great, intense flavor, as well as structural integrity. Top with avocado slices for some healthy fat and serve with homemade Sweet Potato & Carrot Fries (page 40) for one heck of a meal!

Cooking spray

1 can (15 ounces, or 425 g) chickpeas, rinsed and drained

1 cup (191 g) Quinoa-Lentil Blend (page 18)

1 cup (225 g) sweet peas, canned or (130 g) frozen and thawed

1 egg

½ cup (60 g) chickpea flour or (63 g) all-purpose flour

½ cup (56 g) almond meal

2 tablespoons (30 g) ranch dressing, plus more for serving

1½ teaspoons Montreal Chicken Seasoning

1 tablespoon (15 ml) Buffalo sauce, plus more for serving

2 teaspoons (7 g) yellow mustard

6 hamburger buns

2 cups (60 g) fresh baby spinach

3 avocados, peeled, pitted, and sliced

Preheat the oven to 375°F (190°C, or gas mark 5). Spray a baking sheet with nonstick cooking spray and set aside.

In a medium bowl, mash the chickpeas with a fork or use an immersion blender.

Stir in the Quinoa-Lentil Blend, peas, egg, flour, almond meal, ranch dressing, Montreal Chicken Seasoning, Buffalo sauce, and mustard. Form the mixture into 6 patties and place them in a single layer on the prepared sheet. Bake for 40 minutes, flipping halfway through.

Serve on hamburger buns, topped with spinach and avocado slices and extra ranch and Buffalo sauce, if desired.

YIELD: 6 BURGERS

4

Tasty Beef

Loaded Taco Salad with Avocado-Catalina Dressing

Regular purchased French dressing (a.k.a. "catalina") is drowning in sugar and artificial dyes. No wonder kids love it! I created a completely natural whole-food variety that is lower in sugar and yet boasts that sweet tangy flavor that makes the purchased version so irresistible. This is one of our weekly go-to meals!

FOR DRESSING:

½ cup (120 g) organic ketchup

½ cup (120 ml) extra-virgin olive oil

⅓ cup (115 g) raw honey

¼ cup (60 ml) red wine vinegar

½ of an avocado

1 tablespoon (15 ml) Worcestershire sauce

1 teaspoon paprika

1 teaspoon onion powder

Sea salt

Pepper

FOR TACO MEAT:

1 tablespoon (15 ml) extra-virgin olive oil

1 pound (455 g) ground beef

1 cup (100 g) finely chopped cauliflower

½ cup (120 ml) water

¼ cup (30 g) taco seasoning

FOR SALAD:

2 heads of romaine lettuce, chopped

1 can (15 ounces, or 425 g) black beans, heated

1 roasted red bell pepper, diced

8 grape tomatoes, sliced

1 avocado, sliced

½ cup (58 g) shredded Colby Jack cheese

2 tablespoons (2 g) fresh cilantro

1 cup (26 g) tortilla chips, broken into pieces

TO MAKE THE AVOCADO-CATALINA DRESSING: In a large glass measuring cup, combine the ketchup, olive oil, honey, red wine vinegar, avocado, Worcestershire sauce, paprika, and onion powder. Using an immersion blender, or in a food processor, blend until smooth. Season to taste with sea salt and pepper. Set aside.

TO MAKE THE TACO MEAT: In a large pan over medium-high heat, heat the olive oil. Add the ground beef and cauliflower. Cook for about 8 minutes, stirring frequently until the beef is crumbled and no longer pink. Stir in the water and taco seasoning and cook or about 3 minutes more until heated through.

TO ASSEMBLE THE SALAD: Fill your bowl with romaine lettuce. Top with the taco meat, black beans, roasted red bell pepper, tomatoes, avocado, Colby Jack cheese, cilantro, and tortilla chips. Finish with the Avocado-Catalina Dressing.

YIELD: 4 SERVINGS

✳ EXTRA AVOCADO-CATALINA DRESSING

The extra dressing can be refrigerated in an airtight container for up to 1 week. It's also delicious as a dip for carrots or sugar snap peas!

Mexican Tortilla Pie

This savory pie is filled with seasoned beef, shredded sweet potato, spinach, and cheese. But, the crispy tortilla crust is what really makes this dish!

1 tablespoon (15 ml) extra-virgin olive oil

1 pound (455 g) ground beef

1 cup (133 g) grated sweet potato

2 tablespoons (15 g) taco seasoning

9 small flour tortillas, divided

1 cup (30 g) fresh baby spinach

1 can (15 ounces, or 425 g) green chile sauce, divided

1½ cups (173 g) shredded Cheddar Jack cheese, divided

½ cup (130 g) salsa

⅔ cup (154 g) plain Greek yogurt

Preheat the oven to 375°F (190°C, or gas mark 5).

In a large nonstick sauté pan or skillet over medium-high heat, heat the olive oil. Add the ground beef and sweet potato and cook for about 5 minutes until the meat is mostly browned. Stir in the taco seasoning and then remove from the heat.

Line the bottom of a 9-inch (23 cm) deep pie dish with 3 tortillas in a single layer. Tear some in half, as needed, to fill any gaps. Spread the spinach evenly over the tortillas. Sprinkle with 1 cup (120 g) of the Cheddar Jack cheese and top with half of the green chile sauce. Layer on 3 more tortillas in a single layer. Gently press down on the layers to make room for the remaining ingredients.

Next, spoon on the meat and sweet potato mixture, followed by the remaining half of the green chile sauce. Top with the 3 remaining tortillas covering the top completely and sprinkle on the remaining ½ cup (60 g) of Cheddar Jack cheese.

Bake for 20 minutes. The cheese should be bubbly and lightly browned on top.

Serve hot with the salsa and Greek yogurt.

YIELD: 6 SERVINGS

Cauliflower Meatballs over Zoodles

Hands-down, this is our favorite meatball recipe. And I've eaten a lot of meatballs over the last 35 years—my dad is Italian! These are the perfect texture and full of nourishing superfoods that you wouldn't normally expect, such as cauliflower and avocado. If you don't have zucchini to make zoodles, this dish would be fabulous over regular pasta, as well.

FOR MEATBALLS:

1 pound (455 g) ground beef

1 cup (100 g) very finely diced cauliflower

1 egg

½ of an avocado, mashed

½ cup (60 g) Italian bread crumbs

2 teaspoons dried basil

1 teaspoon dried oregano

½ teaspoon sea salt

½ teaspoon pepper

2 tablespoons (28 ml) extra-virgin olive oil

FOR ZOODLES:

2 tablespoons (28 ml) extra-virgin olive oil

2 large zucchini, spiralized (about 8 cups [960 g] zoodles)

2 cups (500 g) organic spaghetti sauce

½ cup (50 g) grated Parmesan cheese

Sea salt

Pepper

TO MAKE THE MEATBALLS: In a large bowl, combine the ground beef, cauliflower, egg, avocado, bread crumbs, basil, oregano, sea salt, and pepper. With your hands, knead the beef mixture, making sure everything is thoroughly combined. Form the mixture into 16 meatballs, about 1½ inches (3.5 cm) in size.

In a large skillet over medium-high heat, heat the olive oil. Cook 8 meatballs at a time, placing them in a circle along the outer 2 inches (5 cm) of the pan. Cook each side of the meatball for about 2 minutes, turning it to cook the other sides and getting all sides evenly browned. Total cook time is about 8 minutes for each batch. Remove the meatballs from the skillet, set aside, and repeat with the remaining 8 meatballs.

TO MAKE THE ZOODLES: While cooking the last batch of meatballs, in another large skillet over medium heat, heat the olive oil. Add the zucchini noodles and sauté for about 5 minutes until softened but not mushy. Stir in the spaghetti sauce and heat until warm.

TO SERVE: Layer 2 cups (about 240 g) of zoodles with sauce into each bowl. Top with 3 to 4 meatballs and sprinkle with Parmesan cheese. Season to taste with sea salt and pepper. Serve hot.

YIELD: 4 SERVINGS

Buffalo-Ranch Sloppy Joes

Everyone loves sloppy Joes. Here, the sweet potato, carrots, and quinoa boost the nutrition and blend perfectly with the ground beef to create the base. You can also substitute ground chicken, if you prefer. This meal is kid-friendly and not too spicy. If you like things spicier, add another tablespoon (15 ml) of Buffalo sauce!

1 pound (455 g) ground beef

½ cup (67 g) shredded sweet potato

¼ cup (28 g) shredded carrot

1 cup (245 g) tomato sauce

½ cup (96 g) Quinoa-Lentil Blend (page 18)

¼ cup (65 g) barbecue sauce

2 tablespoons (28 ml) Buffalo sauce (or more if you like things spicier!)

¼ teaspoon sea salt

¼ teaspoon pepper

4 hamburger buns

¼ cup (60 g) ranch dressing, divided

In a large skillet over medium-high heat, place the ground beef, sweet potato, and carrot. Cook for about 5 minutes until the meat is crumbled and browned.

Add the tomato sauce, Quinoa-Lentil Blend, barbecue sauce, Buffalo sauce, sea salt, and pepper. Stir to combine. Reduce the heat to medium and simmer for 25 minutes, stirring frequently.

Serve warm on hamburger buns and top each with 1 tablespoon (15 g) of ranch dressing.

YIELD: 4 SERVINGS

✳ RECIPE PAIRINGS

These sloppy Joes pair well with Sweet Potato & Carrot Fries (page 40) to round out the meal.

Mini Meatloaves

Meatloaf is one of our favorite meals—it's like a burger and a bun combined into one! Usually meatloaf takes over an hour to cook, but baking it in individual muffin cups helps them cook through much more quickly. There's no need to wait for the weekend—this comforting meal can be had any weeknight now! Serve with your favorite green vegetable and a big scoop of mashed potatoes on the side.

FOR MEATLOAF:
Cooking spray
1 pound (455 g) ground beef
1 egg
⅔ cup (127 g) Quinoa-Lentil Blend (page 18)
2 tablespoons (14 g) almond flour
2 tablespoons (30 g) organic ketchup
2 tablespoons (31 g) garlic hummus or regular hummus
1 tablespoon (15 ml) Worcestershire sauce
1½ teaspoons Montreal Steak Seasoning

FOR SAUCE:
⅓ cup (80 g) organic ketchup
2 tablespoons (18 g) coconut sugar
¼ teaspoon ground mustard

Preheat the oven to 400°F (200°C, or gas mark 6). Spray a 12-cup muffin tin with nonstick cooking spray and set aside.

TO MAKE THE MEATLOAF: In a large bowl, combine the ground beef, egg, Quinoa-Lentil Blend, almond flour, ketchup, hummus, Worcestershire sauce, and Montreal Steak Seasoning. Use your hands to knead the beef mixture, making sure everything is thoroughly combined. Divide the meatloaf mixture among the muffins cups, filling each cup almost to the top. You will use about 10 of the 12 muffin cups.

TO MAKE THE SAUCE: In a small bowl, stir together the ketchup, coconut sugar, and ground mustard. Spoon a little sauce over each mini meatloaf.

Bake the meatloaves for 25 minutes or until the beef is cooked through and no longer pink. Serve warm with sides of your choice.

YIELD: 10 MINI MEATLOAVES

Note: You can form the meat into one giant loaf to cook, as well, but you will need more time for it to bake—between 50 and 60 minutes.

✳ GIVE IT A TWIST: PINEAPPLE TERIYAKI MEATLOAF

Here's a tropical twist on a classic: Add ½ cup (80 g) diced pineapple to the meatloaf mixture. Cook as directed and then drizzle with this teriyaki sauce: In a small bowl, whisk together ¼ cup (60 ml) teriyaki sauce, 2 tablespoons (28 ml) pineapple juice, 1 teaspoon soy sauce, 1 teaspoon molasses, and 1 tablespoon (6 g) of almond flour.

Autumn Harvest Chili

Get even your picky kids (or spouse!) to eat tons of veggies, without complaining or negotiating, with this delicious fall chili—and sneak in a few more when you serve it with Superfood Cornbread Muffins (page 108)! Spinach, orange bell pepper, chickpeas, pumpkin purée, tomatoes, apples, black-eyed peas, corn . . . I feel healthier just talking about it!

1 tablespoon (15 ml) extra-virgin olive oil

1 tablespoon (10 g) minced garlic

2 cups (60 g) fresh baby spinach

1 orange bell pepper, stemmed, seeded, and diced

1 apple, diced

¼ of a yellow onion, diced

1 pound (455 g) ground beef

2 quarts (2 L) organic chicken broth or vegetable broth

2 cans (15 ounces, or 425 g each) diced tomatoes

2 cans (15 ounces, or 425 g each) black-eyed peas, rinsed and drained

1 can (15 ounces, or 425 g) chickpeas, rinsed and drained

¾ cup (123 g) organic frozen sweet corn kernels or (158 g) canned corn

⅓ cup (82 g) pure pumpkin purée (not pumpkin pie filling with sugar and spices)

2½ tablespoons (19 g) chili powder

1 tablespoon (10 g) Montreal Steak Seasoning

1 tablespoon (20 g) molasses

1 tablespoon (20 g) raw honey

Superfood Cornbread Muffins (page 108) (optional)

In a large stockpot over medium-high heat, heat the olive oil. Add the garlic and stir until fragrant, about 30 seconds. Stir in the spinach, orange bell pepper, apple, and onion. Cook for about 5 minutes until the bell pepper is softened. Remove these veggies from the stockpot and set aside.

Return the pot to medium-high heat and add the ground beef. Cook for about 5 minutes until the meat is crumbled and browned. Stir in the sautéed veggies.

Add the chicken broth, tomatoes, black-eyed peas, chickpeas, corn, pumpkin, chili powder, Montreal Steak Seasoning, molasses, and honey. Stir to combine. Reduce the heat to simmer and cook for 20 to 30 minutes. Serve warm with the Superfood Cornbread Muffins (if using).

YIELD: 4 SERVINGS

Superfood Cornbread Muffins

These cornbread muffins will become your new favorite—not too dry, but not too dense, either. In addition to the cornmeal, these muffins feature frozen organic sweet corn kernels full of fiber, vitamin C, and magnesium. What an easy way to get in even MORE veggies!

Cooking spray

2 eggs

1 cup (164 g) frozen organic sweet corn kernels

1 cup (235 ml) unsweetened almond milk

⅓ cup (77 g) mashed avocado

¼ cup (60 ml) melted coconut oil

1 tablespoon (20 g) dark amber maple syrup

1½ cups (210 g) cornmeal

1 teaspoon baking powder

½ teaspoon baking soda

¼ teaspoon sea salt

Preheat the oven to 375°F (190°C, or gas mark 5). Coat a 12-cup muffin tin with nonstick cooking spray and set aside.

In a medium bowl, whisk together the eggs, corn, almond milk, avocado, coconut oil, and maple syrup until thoroughly combined.

In a small bowl, mix the cornmeal, baking powder, baking soda, and sea salt. Slowly stir the dry ingredients into the wet ingredients. Spoon the batter evenly into the muffin cups, filling each cup about three-fourths full.

Bake for 25 minutes or until the tops are lightly browned.

YIELD: 12 MUFFINS

Cheeseburger Soup

If you've never heard of this soup, you might be surprised to see pickles and hamburger bun cubes served on top. Don't let it deter you from trying it; you will love these flavors!

1 tablespoon (14 g) butter

1 tablespoon (15 ml) extra-virgin olive oil

1 pound (455 g) ground beef

½ of a sweet potato, diced into ½-inch (1 cm) cubes

½ of a yellow onion, diced

1 tablespoon (15 ml) Worcestershire sauce

1 tablespoon (10 g) Montreal Steak Seasoning

1½ teaspoons minced garlic

1 quart (946 ml) organic chicken broth or vegetable broth

2 cups (475 ml) unsweetened almond milk

8 ounces (225 g) mild Cheddar cheese

½ cup (60 g) plain Greek yogurt

½ cup (96 g) Quinoa-Lentil Blend (page 18)

½ cup (120 g) organic ketchup

½ cup (78 g) diced dill pickles

3 slices of cooked bacon, crumbled

1 hamburger bun top, toasted and diced

In a large stockpot over medium-high heat, heat the butter and olive oil. Add the ground beef, sweet potato, onion, Worcestershire sauce, Montreal Steak Seasoning, and garlic. Cook for about 5 minutes, breaking the beef apart with a spatula as it cooks until the beef is no longer pink and the sweet potatoes and onions are softened.

Stir in the chicken broth, almond milk, Cheddar cheese, Greek yogurt, Quinoa-Lentil Blend, and ketchup. Reduce the heat to simmer and cook for 25 minutes, stirring frequently.

Top each serving with some pickle, bacon, and toasted bun.

YIELD: 4 SERVINGS

Skillet Lasagna

Lasagna doesn't have to come from the freezer section of the grocery store. And it no longer takes an hour or more to cook when you make it on the stovetop and use no-boil noodles! You will love this easy, homemade version for both its taste and ease of preparation.

1 tablespoon (15 ml) extra-virgin olive oil

½ pound (225 g) ground beef

1 cup (100 g) finely diced cauliflower

1 tablespoon (10 g) minced garlic

1 tablespoon (2 g) dried basil

½ teaspoon sea salt

½ teaspoon pepper

½ cup (120 ml) water

½ cup (120 ml) red wine

1 cup (30 g) fresh baby spinach

4 to 6 "no-boil" lasagna noodles, broken into smaller pieces

1¾ cups (438 g) spaghetti sauce

½ cup (115 g) cottage cheese

½ cup (40 g) shredded Parmesan cheese

4 ounces (115 g) fresh mozzarella cheese, thinly sliced

6 fresh basil leaves

In a large oven-safe skillet over medium-high heat, heat the olive oil. Add the ground beef, cauliflower, garlic, basil, sea salt, and pepper. Cook for about 5 minutes until the meat is crumbled and mostly browned. Stir in the water and red wine.

Place the spinach leaves in a single layer on top of the beef, followed by a single layer of lasagna noodle pieces. Pour the spaghetti sauce over, cover the skillet, and reduce the heat to medium-low. Simmer for 15 minutes until the noodles soften.

Heat the oven to broil.

Top the lasagna with dollops of cottage cheese, sprinkles of Parmesan cheese, a single layer of mozzarella cheese slices, and the fresh basil leaves. Put the oven-safe skillet in the oven and broil for 5 minutes until the cheeses melt completely and are lightly browned. Serve hot.

YIELD: 4 TO 6 SERVINGS

Spiced Beef & Hummus Pitas

I must declare, this is my favorite recipe in the entire book!! It's absolutely delicious, a wonderful combination of flavors and textures, and super easy to make—try this one first, or next!

FOR SPICED BEEF:

1 tablespoon (15 ml) extra-virgin olive oil

1 pound (455 g) ground beef

½ cup (96 g) Quinoa-Lentil Blend (page 18)

1 tablespoon (10 g) minced garlic

½ teaspoon ground cinnamon

½ teaspoon ground cumin

½ teaspoon chili powder

¼ teaspoon sea salt

⅛ teaspoon onion powder

⅛ teaspoon cayenne pepper

FOR SAUCE:

⅔ cup (154 g) plain Greek yogurt

¼ cup (35 g) grated cucumber

1 tablespoon (15 ml) fresh lemon juice

FOR SERVING:

4 pita rounds, halved and split open to make a pouch

2 cups (110 g) mixed baby greens (baby spinach, baby kale, and butter lettuce)

⅓ cup (82 g) garlic hummus or regular hummus

4 peppadew peppers, diced

¼ of a red onion, thinly sliced

TO MAKE THE SPICED BEEF: In a large oven-safe skillet over medium-high heat, heat the olive oil. Add the ground beef, Quinoa-Lentil Blend, garlic, cinnamon, cumin, chili powder, sea salt, onion powder, and cayenne pepper. Cook for 5 to 6 minutes until the meat is browned and no pink remains.

TO MAKE THE SAUCE: In a small bowl, mix the Greek yogurt, cucumber, and lemon juice.

TO SERVE: Stuff the pita halves with a handful of greens, a generous spoonful of spiced beef, a dollop of hummus, a dollop of yogurt sauce, a few pieces of peppadew peppers, and some red onion.

YIELD: 8 PITAS, OR 4 SERVINGS

✴ MAKE IT A SALAD

Double the amount of greens and yogurt sauce. Top the greens with the spiced beef and other toppings, dress with the sauce, and serve the pita on the side.

Southwestern Hamburgers with Guac

This guacamole is not only the perfect burger topping, it's also a party-perfect appetizer. It's creamy, tropical, flavorful, super easy to make, and hands-down the best way to make guacamole!

FOR HAMBURGERS:

1½ pounds (680 g) ground beef

½ cup (58 g) shredded Pepper Jack cheese

1 egg

2 tablespoons (14 g) almond flour

1½ tablespoons (25 ml) Worcestershire sauce

1 tablespoon (9 g) diced mild green chiles

1½ teaspoons Montreal Steak Seasoning

1 teaspoon sea salt

FOR GUAC:

2 avocados, halved and pitted

¼ cup (60 g) plain Greek yogurt

¼ cup (43 g) diced fresh peaches or (63 g) frozen and thawed

2 tablespoons (32 g) salsa

1 tablespoon (15 ml) fresh lime juice

1 tablespoon (10 g) diced red onion

1 tablespoon (1 g) minced fresh cilantro

FOR SERVING:

6 hamburger buns

6 slices of cooked bacon (optional)

TO MAKE THE HAMBURGERS: In a large bowl, combine the ground beef, Pepper Jack cheese, egg, almond flour, Worcestershire sauce, green chiles, Montreal Steak Seasoning, and sea salt. Use your hands to knead the beef mixture, making sure everything is thoroughly combined. Form the mixture into 6 equal-size patties.

On an outdoor grill set to high heat or a skillet over high heat, sear the burgers for 2 minutes per side. Then, reduce the heat to medium-low and cook for 3 to 4 minutes more until they are cooked to your liking. (I like mine medium to medium-well.)

TO MAKE THE GUAC: Into a medium bowl, scoop out the avocado flesh. Add the Greek yogurt, peaches, salsa, lime juice, red onion, and cilantro. Use a fork to mash the ingredients together and mix well.

TO SERVE: Place the hot burgers on hamburger buns, topped with the guacamole and bacon (if using).

YIELD: 6 BURGERS

Asian Lettuce Wraps

A little sweet and a little spicy, these lettuce wraps will remind you of your favorite restaurant appetizer.

FOR SAUCE:

⅓ cup (85 g) barbecue sauce

¼ cup (60 ml) extra-virgin olive oil

¼ cup (60 ml) soy sauce

¼ cup (60 ml) rice wine vinegar

¼ cup (60 ml) orange juice

2 tablespoons (30 g) Thai chili paste

2 tablespoons (40 g) raw honey

1 tablespoon (15 ml) toasted sesame oil

FOR MEAT:

1 pound (455 g) ground beef

1 cup (133 g) shredded sweet potato

1 can (8 ounces, or 225 g) water chestnuts, rinsed, drained, and finely diced

½ cup (96 g) Quinoa-Lentil Blend (page 18)

1 tablespoon (10 g) minced garlic

1-inch (2.5 cm) piece of fresh ginger, grated

FOR SERVING:

12 butter lettuce leaves or iceberg lettuce leaves

Diced scallions (optional)

Red pepper flakes (optional)

TO MAKE THE SAUCE: In a large glass measuring cup, mix the barbecue sauce, olive oil, soy sauce, rice wine vinegar, orange juice, Thai chili paste, honey, and sesame oil. Set aside.

TO MAKE THE MEAT: In a large skillet over medium-high heat, combine the ground beef, sweet potato, water chestnuts, Quinoa-Lentil Blend, garlic, and ginger. Cook for about 5 minutes until the meat is browned and no pink remains.

Once the meat is cooked, pour the sauce over and stir so everything is evenly coated. Cook for 3 minutes more until the sauce is warmed through.

TO SERVE: Scoop a generous mixture of the meat into each lettuce leaf. Sprinkle with scallions and red pepper flakes (if using).

YIELD: 4 TO 6 SERVINGS

5

Sensational Seafood

Crispy Honey-Chipotle Shrimp Tacos

These tacos are definitely a little spicy (hello, chipotle peppers!). To make them more kid-friendly, make an extra batch of sauce without the chipotle peppers. They will love the honey and orange combination! You could also add sliced avocado to the finished tacos, if you like, to boost the superfood value even more.

FOR SHRIMP:

½ cup (56 g) quinoa flour

2 eggs

2 tablespoons (28 ml) melted butter

1½ cups (168 g) almond flour

1½ tablespoons (11 g) Old Bay seasoning

1½ teaspoons sea salt

¼ teaspoon pepper

1¼ pounds (570 g) medium shrimp, tails removed, deveined, and thawed

FOR SAUCE:

¼ cup (85 g) raw honey

¼ cup (62 g) diced chipotle peppers in adobo sauce

¼ cup diced (46 g) orange

FOR TACOS:

8 small flour tortillas

2 cups (60 g) fresh baby spinach or chard

1 cup (191 g) Quinoa-Lentil Blend (page 18)

2 tablespoons (30 g) ranch dressing

2 tablespoons (2 g) fresh cilantro leaves

Preheat the oven to 400°F (200°C, or gas mark 6) and line a baking sheet with parchment paper or aluminum foil.

TO MAKE THE HONEY-CHIPOTLE SHRIMP: Line up 3 small bowls on your work surface. In the first bowl, place the quinoa flour. In the second bowl, whisk together the eggs and melted butter. In the third bowl, mix the almond flour, Old Bay seasoning, sea salt, and pepper.

Roll the shrimp in the quinoa flour until completely coated. Then, dip the shrimp into the egg mixture, letting any excess drip off. Then, dunk the shrimp into the seasoned almond flour, making sure to coat all sides completely. Place the shrimp in a single layer on the prepared baking sheet. Bake for 16 minutes or until crispy and golden brown, flipping the shrimp halfway through the baking time.

MEANWHILE, TO MAKE THE HONEY-CHIPOTLE SAUCE: In a small bowl, stir together the honey, chipotle pepper, and orange. If you want to make the sauce a little more kid-friendly, omit the chipotle peppers.

Once the shrimp are done, transfer them to a large bowl. Stir in half to three-fourths of the Honey-Chipotle Sauce until the shrimp are even coated.

IMMEDIATELY ASSEMBLE THE TACOS: Fill a tortilla with spinach. Top with 1 or 2 spoonfuls of the Quinoa-Lentil Blend, some Honey-Chipotle Shrimp, a drizzle of ranch dressing, and a sprinkle of cilantro.

YIELD: 8 TACOS, OR 4 SERVINGS

Citrus BBQ Shrimp with Sweet Potato Hash

I wish it was always summer and grilling season because that's when my husband does more of the cooking! And it's sunnier and warmer and lighter longer into the evening. If it's not summer, you can still make these shrimp on the stovetop.

FOR SHRIMP:

3 tablespoons (60 g) orange marmalade

2 tablespoons (32 g) barbecue sauce

1½ teaspoons extra-virgin olive oil

1 teaspoon Old Bay seasoning

1¼ pounds (570 g) medium shrimp, tails removed, deveined, and thawed

FOR HASH BROWNS:

2 cups (266 g) diced sweet potato

1 cup (100 g) finely diced cauliflower

1 orange bell pepper or red bell pepper, diced

2 tablespoons (28 ml) extra-virgin olive oil

1 tablespoon (20 g) orange marmalade

TO MAKE THE SHRIMP: In a small bowl, stir together the orange marmalade, barbecue sauce, olive oil, and Old Bay seasoning. In a large zipper-top plastic bag, place the shrimp. Pour the marinade over the shrimp, seal the bag, and turn to coat. Place the shrimp into the refrigerator for 30 minutes to marinate. If you're pressed for time, you can skip the marinating time.

Heat the grill (or skillet on the stovetop) to high. Put the shrimp in a nonstick grill basket, or skewer them, and cook for about 10 minutes until opaque, pink, and cooked through, turning as needed.

MEANWHILE, TO MAKE THE HASH BROWNS: In a large sauté pan or skillet over medium-high heat, combine the sweet potato, cauliflower, orange bell pepper, olive oil, and orange marmalade. Cook for 10 minutes, stirring occasionally so the sweet potatoes soften and begin to brown.

TO SERVE: Layer the shrimp over the hash browns.

YIELD: 4 SERVINGS

✳ NO MARMALADE?

Substitute ¼ cup (46 g) diced orange plus 1 tablespoon (20 g) of raw honey mixed together.

Salmon Burgers

Salmon has always been one of my daughter's favorite proteins—even as a toddler. She eats it by itself, in tacos, smoked, in quiche, and now in burger form. These burgers have a sophisticated flavor, yet are kid-friendly at the same time. It's a win-win for the whole family!

FOR SALMON BURGERS:

3 cans (5 ounces, or 140 g each) wild salmon

1 egg

½ cup (96 g) Quinoa-Lentil Blend (page 18)

¼ cup (28 g) almond flour

1 tablespoon (15 g) Greek yogurt

1 teaspoon spicy brown mustard

1 teaspoon dried basil

1 teaspoon Old Bay seasoning

1 hamburger bun, torn into small pieces

2 tablespoons (28 ml) extra-virgin olive oil

FOR SERVING:

6 slices of provolone cheese

6 hamburger buns

⅔ cup (154 g) plain Greek yogurt

Juice of ½ of a lemon

1 cup (55 g) mixed baby greens (baby spinach and butter lettuce are my favorites)

6 slices of bacon (optional)

TO MAKE THE SALMON BURGERS: In a medium bowl, mix the salmon, egg, Quinoa-Lentil Blend, almond flour, Greek yogurt, mustard, basil, Old Bay seasoning, and hamburger bun pieces until well combined. Form the salmon mixture into 6 round patties and place on a plate. Refrigerate for 30 minutes.

In a large skillet over medium heat, heat the olive oil. Add the salmon patties and fry for about 4 minutes per side. The patties should be browned, but not black.

TO SERVE: Place 1 slice of provolone cheese on each salmon burger. Cover and let the cheese melt for 2 to 3 minutes.

Meanwhile, in a small bowl, mix the Greek yogurt and lemon juice.

Place 1 salmon burger on each hamburger bun bottom, top with a spoonful of yogurt sauce, some greens, 1 slice of bacon (if using), and finish with the bun top.

YIELD: 6 SALMON BURGERS

Salmon Salad with Roasted Corn & Tomatoes

My husband is not a big fan of seafood on salad (though everyone else loves and devours it). So, I serve his delicious cooked salmon over a bed of Quinoa-Lentil Blend instead of spinach salad. You can even put it in tacos with Greek yogurt and sliced red cabbage. The flavors here are very versatile!

FOR SALMON

1 cup (164 g) organic frozen corn, thawed

1 cup (180 g) grape tomatoes, sliced

2 peppadew peppers, diced

2 frozen wild salmon fillets (8 ounces, or 225 g each), thawed

1 tablespoon (15 ml) extra-virgin olive oil

1 teaspoon fresh lemon juice

½ teaspoon sea salt

¼ teaspoon pepper

FOR DRESSING:

2 tablespoons (28 ml) extra-virgin olive oil

1 tablespoon (20 g) raw honey

1½ teaspoons chili paste

1½ teaspoons rice vinegar

1½ teaspoons fresh lemon juice

1 teaspoon garlic

FOR SALAD:

6 cups (180 g) fresh baby spinach

1 avocado, peeled, pitted, and sliced

Preheat the oven to 350°F (180°C, or gas mark 4).

TO MAKE THE SALMON: In a small baking dish, place the corn, tomatoes, and peppadew peppers in the bottom. Place the salmon fillets over the vegetables and brush them with olive oil. Sprinkle the lemon juice, sea salt, and pepper evenly over the top. Bake for 30 minutes or until the fish is opaque and cooked through.

MEANWHILE, TO MAKE THE DRESSING: In a large glass measuring cup, whisk together the olive oil, honey, chili paste, rice vinegar, lemon juice, and garlic until thoroughly combined. Set aside.

TO MAKE THE SALADS: Place 2 cups (60 g) of spinach in each bowl. Top each with a few avocado slices and a serving of salmon with some corn, tomatoes, and peppadew peppers. Then, drizzle with a few tablespoons (45 to 60 ml) of dressing (you probably won't need it all) and serve.

YIELD: 3 TO 4 SERVINGS

✳ PEPPADEW PEPPERS

My parents recently introduced our family to the deliciousness of peppadew peppers. They are found in the olive bar at regular grocery stores where you can buy them by the pound. I always make sure to drain off all the liquid/olive oil before purchasing, so I don't have to pay for any extra weight! They add the perfect amount of sweetness and tang to so many dishes—like this salmon salad, the Spinach Pesto Pizza (page 79), and—my favorite—the Spiced Beef & Hummus Pitas (page 115).

Thai Coconut Salmon Salad

The combination of textures in this salad is phenomenal. Crunchy cabbage, coconut, and almonds are combined with soft cucumber, carrots, and salmon and topped with a fabulous almond butter dressing.

FOR SALMON

1 tablespoon (15 ml) extra-virgin olive oil

2 fresh wild salmon fillets (5 ounces, or 140 g each), or frozen and thawed

1 tablespoon (15 g) Thai chili paste

FOR DRESSING:

2 tablespoons (32 g) creamy almond butter

2 tablespoons (28 ml) extra-virgin olive oil

2 tablespoons (28 ml) sesame oil

1 tablespoon (15 ml) rice vinegar

1 tablespoon (20 g) maple syrup

1 tablespoon (10 g) minced garlic

FOR SALAD:

6 cups (180 g) fresh baby spinach

1 cup (90 g) diced green cabbage

1 cup (110 g) grated carrots

½ cup (96 g) Quinoa-Lentil Blend (page 18)

½ cup (70 g) diced cucumber

½ cup (30 g) unsweetened coconut flakes

½ cup (46 g) sliced almonds

TO MAKE THE SALMON: In a large sauté pan over medium-high heat, heat the olive oil. Add the salmon fillets and sear for 3 minutes on one side. Brush the Thai chili paste on the fillets and then flip. Sear the other side for 4 minutes. Flip once more and cook for 2 to 3 minutes more until the salmon is opaque and cooked through. Remove from heat and set aside.

TO MAKE THE DRESSING: In a large glass measuring cup, whisk together the almond butter, olive oil, sesame oil, rice vinegar, maple syrup, and garlic until thoroughly combined. Set aside.

TO MAKE THE SALAD: In a large salad bowl, toss together the spinach, cabbage, carrots, Quinoa-Lentil Blend, cucumber, coconut, and almonds. Pour the dressing over the salad and toss to combine. Portion the salad into 4 individual serving bowls and top each serving with half of a salmon fillet.

YIELD: 4 SERVINGS

Salmon Quesadillas

Mango goes really well with Mexican food, in my opinion, as in these quesadillas and in the Sriracha-Lime-Cauli Tacos (page 85). It especially pairs well with salmon. These quesadillas are fruity, light, and flavorful.

FOR DIPPING SAUCE:

⅔ cup (154 g) plain Greek yogurt

1 clementine

½ of an avocado

1 tablespoon (16 g) barbecue sauce

FOR SALMON:

2 frozen wild salmon fillets (8 ounces, or 225 g each), thawed

½ of a mango, diced

½ cup (77 g) sweet corn kernels

1 tablespoon (15 ml) extra-virgin olive oil

1 tablespoon (20 g) raw honey

1 tablespoon (15 ml) soy sauce

1 teaspoon ground ginger

FOR QUESADILLAS:

4 large tortillas

1½ cups (173 g) shredded Pepper Jack cheese

½ cup (75 g) crumbled goat cheese (optional)

Butter, for cooking

Preheat the oven to 350°F (180°C, or gas mark 4).

TO MAKE THE DIPPING SAUCE: In a large glass measuring cup, combine the Greek yogurt, clementine, avocado, and barbecue sauce. Using an immersion blender, or in a food processor, purée the sauce. Refrigerate until needed.

TO MAKE THE SALMON: Place the salmon fillets in a small baking pan.

In another large glass measuring cup, stir together the mango, corn, olive oil, honey, soy sauce, and ginger. Pour this over the salmon fillets. Bake for 30 minutes or until the fish is opaque and cooked through.

TO MAKE THE QUESADILLAS: Place 2 tortillas on a work surface. Sprinkle each with a large handful of Pepper Jack cheese and then top each with half of the salmon-corn mixture. Sprinkle goat cheese over each (if using) and top with another tortilla.

In a large skillet over medium heat, melt some butter. Carefully transfer 1 quesadilla to the skillet (or assemble it directly in the pan after the butter melts). Spread some more butter on top of the quesadilla. Cook for 3 or 4 minutes per side until the tortilla is golden brown and the cheese is melted. Transfer to a plate to keep warm and repeat, cooking the remaining quesadilla. Slice into triangles and serve with the dipping sauce.

YIELD: 2 QUESADILLAS, OR 4 SERVINGS

Thai Shrimp & Sweet Potato Quesadillas

Perhaps my second favorite recipe in the book (see my favorite on page 115—Spiced Beef & Hummus Pitas!), these quesadillas are unique and delicious. The mashed sweet potato and coconut pair nicely with the spicy shrimp dipped in an almond butter sauce.

FOR SHRIMP:

1 tablespoon (15 ml) extra-virgin olive oil

1 cup (about 125 g) small shrimp, tails removed, deveined, and thawed

1 teaspoon Thai chili paste

FOR DIPPING SAUCE:

¼ cup (60 ml) coconut milk

2 tablespoons (32 g) creamy almond butter

1 tablespoon (15 g) Thai chili paste

1 tablespoon (15 ml) rice vinegar

1 tablespoon (20 g) raw honey

Juice of ½ of a lime

1 teaspoon garlic

1 teaspoon xanthan gum

FOR QUESADILLAS:

4 large tortillas

½ cup cooked (164 g) sweet potato, mashed

1½ cups (173 g) shredded white Cheddar cheese

½ cup (30 g) unsweetened coconut flakes

Butter, for cooking

TO MAKE THE SHRIMP: In a medium sauté pan or skillet over medium-high heat, heat the olive oil. Add the shrimp and Thai chili paste and sauté for 6 to 8 minutes until the shrimp are opaque and cooked through.

TO MAKE THE DIPPING SAUCE: In a small saucepan on low heat, stir together the coconut milk, almond butter, Thai chili paste, rice vinegar, honey, lime juice, garlic, and xanthan gum. Cook for 4 minutes, stirring constantly until thickened. Set aside while you assemble the quesadillas.

TO MAKE THE QUESADILLAS: Place 2 tortillas on a work surface. Spread each with half of the mashed sweet potato. Sprinkle each with a large handful of Cheddar cheese. Top each with half of the shrimp and coconut shreds and another handful of Cheddar cheese. Then top with another tortilla.

In a large skillet over medium heat, melt some butter. Carefully transfer 1 quesadilla to the skillet (or assemble it directly in the pan after the butter melts). Spread some more butter on top of the quesadilla. Cook for 3 or 4 minutes per side until the tortilla is golden brown and the cheese is melted. Transfer to a plate to keep warm and repeat, cooking the remaining quesadilla. Slice into triangles and serve with the dipping sauce.

YIELD: 2 QUESADILLAS, OR 4 SERVINGS

Not Your Momma's Tuna Casserole

There's nothing ordinary or boring about this tuna casserole. It has a new level of sophistication, while still being easy to make.

Cooking spray

2 cups (60 g) fresh baby spinach

8 ounces (225 g) quinoa pasta, cooked according to the package directions

2 cans (7 ounces, or 200 g each) water-packed albacore tuna

1 can (15 ounces, or 425 g) organic cream of chicken soup

1 cup (130 g) frozen peas, thawed

1 cup (115 g) shredded white Cheddar cheese

½ cup (40 g) shredded Parmesan cheese

½ cup (120 ml) unsweetened almond milk

2 tablespoons (14 g) almond flour

1½ teaspoons extra-virgin olive oil

1 teaspoon minced garlic

1 teaspoon Old Bay seasoning

1 teaspoon Worcestershire sauce

Sea salt

Pepper

12 butter crackers, crushed

Preheat the oven to 400°F (200°C, or gas mark 6). Spray a 9 x 13-inch (23 x 33 cm) glass baking dish with nonstick cooking spray and set aside.

In a large bowl, combine the spinach, quinoa pasta, tuna, cream of chicken soup, peas, Cheddar and Parmesan cheeses, almond milk, almond flour, olive oil, garlic, Old Bay seasoning, and Worcestershire sauce. Season to taste with sea salt and pepper. Stir until thoroughly mixed.

Transfer the casserole mixture to the prepared dish. Top with the crushed crackers. Bake for 30 minutes and serve immediately.

YIELD: 6 SERVINGS

Cauli-Tuna Melts

Have you heard of cauliflower "steaks"? A whole head of cauliflower can be sliced into thick rounds (or "steaks") and then roasted or baked. Here, they add a great flavor and heartiness to these tuna melts.

FOR CAULI STEAKS:

1 head of cauliflower, sliced into ¾-inch-thick (2 cm) rounds

2 tablespoons (28 ml) extra-virgin olive oil

¼ teaspoon sea salt

⅛ teaspoon pepper

FOR TUNA MIXTURE:

1 cup (191 g) Quinoa-Lentil Blend (page 18)

1 can (7 ounces, or 200 g) water-packed albacore tuna

¼ cup (60 g) olive oil mayonnaise

¼ cup (60 g) plain Greek yogurt

2 tablespoons (30 g) sweet relish

1 tablespoon (9 g) diced peppadew peppers

FOR SERVING:

4 English muffins, split

8 slices of provolone cheese

Preheat the oven to 425°F (220°C, or gas mark 7). Line a baking sheet with parchment paper.

TO MAKE THE CAULI STEAKS: Place the cauliflower rounds in a single layer on the prepared sheet. Brush with olive oil and sprinkle with the sea salt and pepper. Bake for 20 minutes or until the cauliflower is lightly browned.

TO MAKE THE TUNA MIXTURE: In a medium bowl, stir together the Quinoa-Lentil Blend, tuna, mayonnaise, Greek yogurt, relish, and peppadew peppers. Set aside.

Reduce the oven temperature to 350°F (180°C, or gas mark 4).

TO ASSEMBLE THE MELTS: Place the English muffin halves on a work surface. Top each with 1 slice of roasted cauliflower, then with a generous spoonful of the tuna mixture, and finally with 1 slice of provolone cheese. Carefully transfer the muffins to the prepared sheet and bake for 10 minutes or until the cheese melts. Serve hot.

YIELD: 8 MELTS, OR 4 SERVINGS

✹ CAULIFLOWER STEAKS

The larger the head of cauliflower is, the better! Cut the full cauliflower in half first, and then cut thick strips (steaks) from each side. Some florets will fall off—that's ok. You can eat those extra non-steak pieces raw or throw them into a smoothie like the Orange Dream Milkshake on page 155.

Quinoa & Crab Corn Chowder

This chowder is one of our favorite soups and makes great leftovers for lunch at work or another dinner later in the week. You can use canned crab, which is very finely shredded, or substitute lump crab cut it into bite-size chunks.

2 tablespoons (28 ml) extra-virgin olive oil

1 tablespoon (10 g) minced garlic

1 cup (133 g) finely diced sweet potato

1 cup (67 g) diced lacinato kale

1 carrot, thinly sliced

1 quart (946 ml) organic chicken broth or vegetable broth

3 cans (6 ounces, or 170 g each) wild crabmeat

1 can (16.5 ounces, or 470 g) creamed corn

1 can (15.5 ounces, or 440 g) organic sweet kernel corn, rinsed and drained

1 cup (191 g) Quinoa-Lentil Blend (page 18)

1 cup (235 ml) unsweetened almond milk

Juice of ½ of a lemon

2 tablespoons (14 g) almond flour

1 tablespoon Old Bay seasoning

¼ teaspoon pepper

French bread, for serving

In a large stockpot over medium-high heat, heat the olive oil. Add the garlic, sweet potato, kale, and carrot. Sauté for about 5 minutes or until the veggies are softened.

Stir in the chicken broth, crabmeat, creamed corn, sweet corn, Quinoa-Lentil Blend, almond milk, lemon juice, almond flour, Old Bay seasoning, and pepper. Reduce the heat to simmer and cook for 25 minutes.

Serve with French bread for dipping.

YIELD: 4 SERVINGS

✳ DON'T LIKE CRAB?

This is fabulous as a salmon chowder too! Cook 2 salmon fillets per the instructions for the Thai Coconut Salmon Salad (page 126) and then flake the fish and add it to the soup!

Lemon-Bourbon Salmon Tacos

This recipe is a twist on a blog and cookbook favorite, my honey-sesame fish tacos. In this new version, I combine honey-bourbon and citrus with salmon to create something truly unique. If salmon is not available, cod works equally as well for a really delicious meal.

FOR SALMON FILLING:

2 tablespoons (28 ml) extra-virgin olive oil

12 ounces (340 g) fresh wild salmon fillets or frozen and thawed

½ cup (96 g) Quinoa-Lentil Blend (page 18)

2 tablespoons (28 ml) honey-bourbon or 2 tablespoons (28 ml) bourbon plus 1 tablespoon (20 g) raw honey

1 tablespoon (20 g) molasses

1 teaspoon minced garlic

1 teaspoon Old Bay seasoning

Juice of ½ of a lemon

FOR SAUCE:

½ cup (115 g) plain Greek yogurt

Juice of ½ of a lemon

FOR SERVING:

8 small flour tortillas

1 roasted red bell pepper, sliced

1 cup (70 g) thinly shredded red cabbage

TO MAKE THE SALMON FILLING: In a large skillet over medium-high heat, heat the olive oil. Add the salmon and sear for 3 minutes per side. Reduce the heat to medium.

Stir in the Quinoa-Lentil Blend, honey-bourbon, molasses, garlic, Old Bay seasoning, and lemon juice. Cook for 5 minutes more and then start flaking the fish, breaking it into smaller pieces so each can be coated evenly with the sauce. The fish should be opaque and cooked through.

TO MAKE THE SAUCE: In a small bowl, stir together the Greek yogurt and lemon juice. Set aside.

TO MAKE THE TACOS: Fill each tortilla with some salmon filling, a few slices of roasted red bell pepper, and a handful of red cabbage. Drizzle with the sauce and serve.

YIELD: 8 TACOS

✸ NON-ALCOHOLIC VERSION

Though most of the alcohol cooks off when used this way, some people prefer not to use alcohol of any kind. If that's the case, substitute the following for the honey-bourbon in this recipe: Mix 1 tablespoon (15 ml) of vanilla extract, plus 1 tablespoon (20 g) of raw honey, plus 1 tablespoon (15 ml) sparkling apple cider.

6

Breakfast for Dinner

Breakfast Berry Cobbler

Your family is going to love this dessert-for-breakfast-for-dinner idea. Berry cobbler for breakfast?! Oh yes, when it includes tons of everyday superfoods like quinoa, blueberries, olive oil, walnuts, and Greek yogurt!

2 cups (290 g) fresh organic wild blueberries or (310 g) frozen and thawed

1 cup (170 g) diced fresh strawberries

1 cup (80 g) rolled oats

½ cup (96 g) Quinoa-Lentil Blend (page 18)

½ cup (56 g) almond flour

½ cup (60 g) coarsely chopped walnuts

¼ cup (28 g) ground flaxseed

¼ cup (60 ml) extra-virgin olive oil

¼ cup (80 g) dark amber maple syrup

¼ cup (60 ml) unsweetened almond milk

1 teaspoon vanilla extract

¼ teaspoon ground cinnamon

1 cup (230 g) plain Greek yogurt

1 tablespoon (20 g) raw honey

Preheat the oven to 375°F (190°C, or gas mark 5).

In a 9 x 9-inch (23 x 23 cm) baking dish, pour the blueberries and strawberries into the bottom.

In a large bowl, stir together the oats, Quinoa-Lentil Blend, almond flour, walnuts, flaxseed, olive oil, maple syrup, almond milk, vanilla, and cinnamon until thoroughly combined. Spread the cobbler mixture evenly over the berries.

Bake for 30 minutes until lightly browned and crispy on top.

Serve hot with a dollop of Greek yogurt and a drizzle of honey.

YIELD: 4 TO 6 SERVINGS

✳ MAKE IT DESSERT!

Instead of topping with Greek yogurt, transform this dish into a true dessert by serving it with a scoop of vanilla ice cream.

Sweet Potato Noodle & Egg Tacos with Citrus Guac

This is another one of my favorite recipes in this entire book! The crispy sweet potato noodles are the perfect balance to the soft, perfectly scrambled eggs . . . and that citrus guac?!?! Oh my goodness, you will want to eat it by the spoonful—and a nutritional spoonful it is.

FOR NOODLES:

1 sweet potato, spiralized or
  julienned

1½ teaspoons extra-virgin olive oil

1 teaspoon paprika

1 teaspoon sea salt

FOR CITRUS GUAC:

2 avocados

2 tablespoons (30 g) Greek yogurt

2 tablespoons (32 g) salsa

2 tablespoons (20 g) diced red
  onion

2 tablespoons (23 g) diced orange

FOR TACOS:

1 teaspoon extra-virgin olive oil

6 eggs

8 small flour tortillas

½ cup (58 g) shredded Colby Jack
  cheese (optional)

3 slices of bacon, cooked and
  crumbled (optional)

Preheat the oven to 425°F (220°C, or gas mark 7).

TO MAKE THE NOODLES: In a medium bowl, mix the sweet potato noodles, olive oil, paprika, and sea salt until the sweet potato noodles are evenly coated.

On a parchment paper–lined baking sheet, spread the noodles in a single layer. Bake for 15 minutes until the noodles get slightly crispy, but not blackened or burned.

MEANWHILE, TO MAKE THE CITRUS GUAC: In a small bowl, use a fork to mash together the avocados, Greek yogurt, salsa, red onion, and orange. Set aside.

TO MAKE THE TACOS: In a small pan over medium-low heat, heat the olive oil. Add the eggs and scramble them, stirring frequently so they do not stick to the bottom of the pan. Cook until your desired doneness.

TO ASSEMBLE THE TACOS: Fill a tortilla with some scrambled eggs. Top with some sweet potato noodles, a spoonful of guac, and a sprinkle of Colby Jack cheese and bacon (if using).

YIELD: 8 TACOS, OR 4 SERVINGS

Green Smoothie Pancakes

Just imagine all the goodness packed into a healthy green smoothie (like the Almond-Mocha Green Smoothie [page 151]), but delivered in pancake form! This is THE most requested breakfast, and breakfast-for-dinner, at our house. Try it and see if it doesn't achieve the same status at yours.

2 cups (60 g) fresh baby spinach

1 small banana

¾ cup (175 ml) unsweetened almond milk

1 tablespoon (20 g) maple syrup

1 tablespoon (16 g) almond butter

1 tablespoon (7 g) ground flaxseed

1 teaspoon vanilla extract

1 cup (120 g) pancake mix

Syrup of choice, for serving

In a large glass measuring cup, place the spinach, banana, almond milk, maple syrup, almond butter, flaxseed, and vanilla. Using an immersion blender, purée until smooth. Stir in the pancake mix.

In a large pan over medium-low heat, pour the batter into small circles, about 3 to 4 inches (7.5 to 10 cm) in diameter. When the pancakes start bubbling a bit and the bottom is slightly browned, flip them. Continue cooking for 1 to 2 minutes on the other side.

Serve warm with your favorite syrup.

YIELD: 9 TO 10 PANCAKES, DEPENDING ON SIZE

✳ MAKE YOUR OWN PANCAKE MIX

If you don't want to buy a premade pancake mix or don't have any on hand, just combine 1 cup (125 g) of whole-wheat flour, 2 teaspoons (9 g) of baking powder, and 1 teaspoon of coconut sugar as a handy substitute.

Sweet Potato Pancakes

These pancakes are sweet, flavorful, and fantastically fluffy. You can eat them plain, with a dollop of nut butter, or covered in syrup—however you like!

½ of a sweet potato

1 cup (235 ml) unsweetened almond milk

½ cup (96 g) Quinoa-Lentil Blend (page 18)

¼ cup (85 g) raw honey

2 eggs

1 cup (125 g) white whole-wheat flour

1 teaspoon ground cinnamon

½ teaspoon baking powder

¼ teaspoon ground ginger

¼ teaspoon ground cloves

1 tablespoon (14 g) butter or coconut oil

1 banana, sliced

¼ cup (23 g) almond slices

Maple syrup, for serving

Microwave the sweet potato for 4 minutes on high and then carefully peel off the skin.

In a high-speed blender, combine the almond milk, Quinoa-Lentil Blend, sweet potato, and honey. Blend until smooth. Pour the purée into a large bowl and then whisk in the eggs.

In a small bowl, combine the flour, cinnamon, baking powder, ginger, and ground cloves. Stir until thoroughly mixed.

Slowly stir the flour mixture into the sweet potato purée, adding about one-third at a time and stirring well to combine.

In a large pan over medium-low heat, melt the butter. Pour the batter into small circles, about 3 to 4 inches (7.5 to 10 cm) in diameter. When the pancakes start bubbling a bit and the bottom is slightly browned, flip them. Continue cooking 1 to 2 minutes on the other side.

Serve warm with banana slices, sliced almonds, and maple syrup.

YIELD: 9 TO 10 PANCAKES, DEPENDING ON SIZE

> ☀ **DIPPING VERSUS DROWNING**
>
> I've found that Babycakes consumes significantly less maple syrup if I cook her silver dollar–size pancakes that she can then dip by hand into the syrup. Otherwise, she's begging me multiple times during breakfast to pour more syrup on top of her already drowning pancakes. Try it with your kids (or adults!)—use small ramekins or dipping bowls.

Triple Chocolate Muffins

Chocolate almond milk, dark chocolate chips, and cocoa powder give these muffins their decadence! Banana, avocado, and eggs give them their powerful nutritional boost and are the reason I feel okay giving my daughter chocolate at breakfast.

Cooking spray or coconut oil

2 eggs

1 medium banana

1 avocado

½ cup (120 ml) chocolate almond milk

½ cup (72 g) coconut sugar

1 teaspoon vanilla extract

1½ cups (188 g) white whole-wheat flour

¼ cup (22 g) cocoa powder

1 teaspoon baking powder

¼ teaspoon sea salt

¾ cup (131 g) chocolate chips

Preheat the oven to 375°F (190°C, or gas mark 5). Spray a 12-cup muffin tin with nonstick cooking spray and set aside.

In a large glass measuring cup, combine the eggs, banana, avocado, chocolate almond milk, coconut sugar, and vanilla. Using an immersion blender, purée until smooth.

In a large bowl, stir together the flour, cocoa powder, baking powder, and sea salt until thoroughly mixed.

Slowly stir the wet ingredients into the dry ingredients. Fold in the chocolate chips.

Spoon the batter evenly into the prepared muffin tin, filling each cup about two-thirds full. Bake for 30 minutes or until a toothpick inserted into the middle comes out clean.

YIELD: 12 MUFFINS, OR 6 SERVINGS

✳ WHAT TO PUT ON TOP

My husband is a traditionalist when it comes to muffins and prefers them sliced in half with a bit of plain ol' butter. But, my daughter and I like to take things to the next level by drizzling each half with melted almond butter. The chocolate and nut butter combination is to die for!

Loaded Avocado Toast

If you've never had baked eggs before, prepare to be amazed! They cook so perfectly, store nicely in the fridge, and transport easily to work or school. As for this toast, the flavors and textures are so delicious that you may never eat boring toast with jam again!

Cooking spray

8 eggs

1½ teaspoons extra-virgin olive oil

4 cups (120 g) fresh baby spinach

1½ teaspoons minced garlic

8 slices of toast

3 avocados, peeled, pitted, and sliced

⅓ cup (41 g) coarsely chopped pistachios

2 teaspoons (5 g) paprika

1 lime, halved

2 tablespoons (2 g) fresh cilantro leaves

Sea salt

Pepper

Preheat the oven to 350°F (180°C, or gas mark 4). Coat 8 cups of a 12-cup muffin tin with nonstick cooking spray.

Crack each egg into a prepared cup. (You can make a full dozen, if you prefer, and save some for later). Bake for 20 to 24 minutes, depending on how firm you like your egg yolks.

Meanwhile, in a large sauté pan or skillet over medium heat, heat the olive oil. Add the spinach and garlic and cook for about 5 minutes or until the spinach is wilting, but not blackened or burnt.

Toast the bread. Top each slice with a spoonful of sautéed spinach, a few slices of avocado in a single layer, about 1½ teaspoons of pistachios, a sprinkle of paprika, a drizzle of lime juice, a few sprigs of cilantro, and, finally, one baked egg. Season to taste with sea salt and pepper.

YIELD: 8 AVOCADO TOASTS

Almond-Mocha Green Smoothie

This smoothie has nut butter, chocolate, and coffee. Do I really need to say more?!? People often ask how many greens should really go into a green smoothie. My answer is: A LOT! You can't really taste them, so you might as well pile them high.

4 cups (120 g) fresh baby spinach

1 frozen banana

½ cup (78 g) frozen organic blueberries

¾ cup (175 ml) unsweetened almond milk

⅓ cup (80 ml) brewed decaf coffee, cooled

2 tablespoons (32 g) almond butter

1 tablespoon (5 g) cocoa powder

1 tablespoon (7 g) ground flaxseed

1 tablespoon (20 g) dark amber maple syrup

1 teaspoon vanilla extract

In a large high-speed blender, combine all ingredients. Blend until smooth, divide between 2 glasses, and serve immediately.

YIELD: 2 (12 OUNCES, OR 355 ML EACH) SERVINGS

✳ BANANA-FREE

Sometimes I leave out the banana completely and use 1½ cups (233 g) of frozen blueberries instead. It definitely makes it a deeper purple/brown color, but I like using them because they are lower on the glycemic index, lower in sugar, and loaded with antioxidants.

Cauliflower & Sweet Potato Hash with Fried Eggs

Really, what's not to love about a big ol' plate of sweet potatoes covered in maple syrup? Paired with fried eggs and diced apple, this dish is the perfect combination of savory and sweet! If you don't have any apples on hand, use an alternative fruit like pears, dried apricots, or golden raisins.

1 tablespoon (15 ml) extra-virgin olive oil

1 tablespoon (14 g) butter

1 medium sweet potato, peeled and diced

1 cup (100 g) finely diced cauliflower

½ cup (75 g) diced apple

2 tablespoons (20 g) diced yellow onion

1 tablespoon (20 g) dark amber maple syrup

¼ teaspoon ground cinnamon

⅛ teaspoon sea salt, plus more to taste

4 eggs

Pepper

In a large skillet over medium-high heat, melt the butter and olive oil. Add the sweet potato, cauliflower, apple, and onion. Sauté for about 8 minutes until the sweet potatoes are softened.

Stir in the maple syrup and cinnamon and sauté until lightly browned. Transfer the vegetables to a serving bowl. Place the skillet back over medium-high heat (no need to wipe it out).

Crack the eggs into the hot skillet, cover, and cook for 2 to 3 minutes for a runny yolk or 4 to 5 minutes for a firmer egg. The egg whites should be opaque. Season to taste with sea salt and pepper. Slide the eggs over the hash and serve immediately.

YIELD: 4 SERVINGS

✳ **SERVING SUGGESTIONS**

For the meat lovers in your house, stir some diced ham or bacon into the hash or serve with toasted bread on the side. Either—or both—are delicious!

Orange Dream Milkshake

Have you ever had a smoothie with cauliflower in it? Probably not, but it has a very mild flavor that combines well with the fresh citrus and vanilla flavors!

4 clementines, peeled

½ of a frozen banana

½ cup (50 g) diced cauliflower

½ cup (120 ml) unsweetened almond milk

1 tablespoon (20 g) maple syrup

1 scoop of vanilla protein powder

¾ cup (105 g) unsweetened almond milk ice cubes

¾ cup (105 g) ice cubes

In a large high-speed blender, combine all the ingredients. Blend until smooth, divide between 2 glasses, and serve immediately.

YIELD: 2 (12 OUNCES, OR 355 ML EACH) SERVINGS

✳ IN THE THICK OF THINGS . . .

If you like your milkshakes on the thicker side, add ½ cup (67 g) frozen sweet potato chunks to the mix. Par-cook the sweet potatoes first (for 15 minutes in fully boiling water or for 4 minutes on high in the microwave) and then peel, slice, and freeze.

Super Orange Juice

My daughter has not grown up on juice—purchased or homemade. She prefers almond milk and water to most everything else. However, this juice has become a favorite of hers! It's bursting with flavor, super refreshing, packed with vitamin C and beta-carotene, and perfectly sweet—even with the bell pepper in there.

1 large sweet potato, peeled

2 oranges, peeled

10 carrots, tops removed

1 orange bell pepper, stemmed

1 apple, cored and seeded

Chop all ingredients small enough to fit through your juicer chute. In a high-speed juicer, juice all of the fruits and veggies. Divide among 3 or 4 glasses and serve immediately.

YIELD: 3 TO 4 SERVINGS (12 OUNCES, OR 355 ML EACH)

Greek Egg Muffins

This might be a record: 7 of the 10 everyday superfoods used in one recipe! These muffins are easy to make for a hearty weeknight meal, but they're also easy to store as leftovers and easy to grab for breakfast on a busy morning.

Cooking spray

1 tablespoon (15 ml) extra-virgin olive oil

2 cups (60 g) fresh baby spinach

6 eggs

½ cup (96 g) Quinoa-Lentil Blend (page 18)

½ cup (75 g) crumbled feta cheese

⅓ cup (33 g) finely diced cauliflower

⅓ cup (80 ml) unsweetened almond milk

6 grape tomatoes, diced

6 black olives, diced

1 teaspoon minced garlic

¼ teaspoon sea salt

⅛ teaspoon pepper

Preheat the oven to 375°F (190°C, or gas mark 5). Spray a 12-cup muffin tin with nonstick cooking spray and set aside.

In a large pan over medium heat, heat the olive oil. Add the spinach and sauté for about 5 minutes. The spinach should be soft and wilted, but not browned.

In a large bowl, whisk the eggs. Stir in the Quinoa-Lentil Blend, feta cheese, cauliflower, almond milk, tomatoes, olives, garlic, sea salt, and pepper until thoroughly combined. Add the spinach and stir to combine.

Spoon the batter evenly into the prepared muffin tin, filling each cup about three-fourths full.

Bake for 25 minutes or until the tops are lightly browned.

YIELD: 12 EGG MUFFINS, OR 6 SERVINGS

Chocolate-Orange Muffins

Chocolate and orange make a classic combination for desserts and now for breakfast, too. You will love these light, rich, fluffy muffins any time of day.

Cooking spray

1½ cups (188 g) white whole-wheat flour

2 tablespoons (10 g) cocoa powder

1½ teaspoons baking powder

½ teaspoon sea salt

2 eggs

1 ripe medium banana, mashed

¾ cup (108 g) coconut sugar

½ cup (93 g) diced orange or clementine

¼ cup (60 g) plain Greek yogurt

¼ cup (60 ml) extra-virgin olive oil

¼ cup (60 ml) unsweetened almond milk

1½ teaspoons orange zest

1 teaspoon vanilla extract

Preheat the oven to 375°F (190°C, or gas mark 5). Spray a 12-cup muffin tin with nonstick cooking spray and set aside.

In a medium bowl, stir together the flour, cocoa powder, baking powder, and sea salt until thoroughly mixed. Set aside.

In a large bowl, mix the eggs, banana, coconut sugar, orange, Greek yogurt, olive oil, almond milk, orange zest, and vanilla.

Slowly stir the dry ingredients into the wet ingredients, adding about one-third at a time and stirring well to combine.

Spoon the batter evenly into the prepared muffin tin, filling each cup about three-fourths full.

Bake for 25 minutes or until cooked through.

YIELD: 12 MUFFINS, OR 6 SERVINGS

✳ MAKE-AHEAD OPITON

Often I will bake this recipe as a single loaf the night before and serve it the following morning for breakfast or brunch! Simply let the loaf cool in the loaf pan for 1 hour after baking (adjust the baking time, as needed), cover it with foil, and refrigerate overnight. It makes slicing the bread much easier and makes mornings a breeze!

7

Superfood Desserts

Chocolate-Avocado Bark with Orange Zest and Almonds

This isn't just a dessert full of empty calories. There are actually nourishing ingredients here that also happen to taste amazing together. Both the shredded coconut and avocado add healthy fats that help satisfy you, the almonds help stabilize blood sugar, the orange zest adds vitamin C, and the higher-percentage chocolate is full of antioxidants.

FOR BARK:

3 cups (525 g) dark chocolate chips (62 percent cacao or higher is recommended)

1 medium avocado, mashed

1 tablespoon (15 ml) orange juice

1 tablespoon (6 g) orange zest

1 teaspoon raw honey

FOR TOPPINGS:

2 tablespoons (12 g) sliced almonds, toasted (see sidebar)

2 tablespoons (8 g) unsweetened coconut flakes

1 tablespoon (6 g) orange zest

¼ teaspoon sea salt

Preheat the oven to 400°F (200°C, or gas mark 6). Line a baking sheet with parchment paper and set aside.

TO MAKE THE BARK: Melt the chocolate chips over a double boiler filled with simmering water. Once melted, stir in the avocado, orange juice, orange zest, and honey. Mix thoroughly.

Pour the chocolate mixture onto the prepared sheet. Use a spoon to flatten and level it.

TO ADD THE TOPPINGS: Sprinkle the toasted almonds, coconut, orange zest, and sea salt evenly over the top of the chocolate, pressing them down gently with your hand or the back of a spoon. Refrigerate for 1 hour and then break the bark into pieces and enjoy!

YIELD: ABOUT 36 PIECES

✳ TOASTING ALMONDS

To toast the almonds, place them in a roasting pan or on a rimmed baking sheet and toast in a 400°F (200°C, or gas mark 6) oven for 6 minutes. Remove and set aside to cool.

Meyer Lemon Bars

A rich, buttery, cookie-like crust is topped with a thick luscious lemon layer that is both sweet and tart. These bars are naturally gluten-free and delish!

FOR CRUST:

Cooking spray

1 cup (112 g) almond flour

⅓ cup (64 g) raw cane sugar

¼ cup (60 ml) extra-virgin olive oil

1 teaspoon xanthan gum

FOR FILLING:

3 eggs

¾ cup (144 g) raw cane sugar

¼ cup (28 g) almond flour

¼ cup (60 ml) fresh Meyer lemon juice or regular lemon juice

Zest of 1 Meyer lemon or regular lemon

¼ cup (30 g) powdered sugar

Preheat the oven to 350°F (180°C, or gas mark 4). Spray a 9 x 9-inch (23 x 23 cm) glass baking dish with nonstick cooking spray and set aside.

TO MAKE THE CRUST: In a medium bowl, stir together the almond flour, cane sugar, olive oil, and xanthan gum until combined. Press the dough evenly into the bottom of the prepared dish and bake for 20 minutes.

MEANWHILE, TO MAKE THE FILLING: In another medium bowl, combine the eggs, cane sugar, almond flour, lemon juice, and lemon zest. With a hand mixer, mix for 2 to 3 minutes on low. Pour the lemon filling over the crust. Return the dish to the oven and bake for 25 minutes more. When done, the lemon layer should be firm, not jiggly.

Remove from the oven, cool the bars completely, and then sprinkle with powdered sugar before serving.

YIELD: 12 TO 16 BARS

✳ WHAT IS XANTHAN GUM?

Xanthan gum is generally used as a gelling agent or thickener—and is required in this recipe as it takes the place of additional butter and sugar in the crust.

Key Lime Pie

Key lime pie is my husband's favorite dessert. So, I have been a woman on a mission to make a more perfect, lower sugar, healthier version of this classic—and I think I've done just that! You be the judge.

¾ cup (75 g) finely diced
   cauliflower

2 cups (475 ml) water

½ cup (120 ml) unsweetened
   almond milk

3 egg yolks

½ cup (115 g) plain Greek yogurt

½ cup (120 ml) fresh key lime juice

½ cup (170 g) raw honey

4 graham cracker sheets
   (16 individual crackers), finely
   crushed

1 store-bought graham cracker
   pie crust

1 cup (235 ml) whipping cream

½ cup (60 g) powdered sugar

Preheat the oven to 350°F (180°C, or gas mark 4).

In a large glass measuring cup, combine the cauliflower and water. Microwave for 2½ minutes on high. Drain out the water.

Pour the almond milk over the cooked cauliflower. Using an immersion blender, purée it.

In a large bowl, stir together the eggs, Greek yogurt, key lime juice, honey, and crushed graham crackers until thoroughly mixed. Pour the filling into the prepared pie crust. Bake for 40 to 45 minutes until a knife inserted in the center comes out clean. Remove from the oven and cool completely.

Once cooled, whip together the whipping cream and powdered sugar. Spread the whipped cream in a thick layer over the top of the pie. Serve cold.

YIELD: 1 (12-INCH [30 CM]) PIE

Pink Chocolate Chip Cookie Dough Balls

This gorgeous pink cookie dough is perfect for the holidays (or anytime for that matter!). It's easy to make, easy to share, and easy to fall in love with. It's completely grain-free (which means it's also gluten-free), dairy-free, vegan, and it has a hidden (or not so hidden) veggie that gives it that beautifully intense color. Be prepared to end up with pink hands, too.

1 medium beet, top removed, peeled

1 teaspoon melted coconut oil

½ cup (160 g) organic strawberry jam

¼ cup (36 g) coconut sugar

2 tablespoons (28 ml) unsweetened almond milk

1 tablespoon (15 ml) extra-virgin olive oil

1 teaspoon vanilla extract

1½ cups (168 g) almond flour

½ cup (56 g) coconut flour

¼ teaspoon sea salt

⅔ cup (117 g) dark chocolate chips

Preheat the oven to 425°F (220°C, or gas mark 7).

Place the beet on a square piece of aluminum foil and top with the coconut oil. Wrap the foil around the beet to enclose it completely. Roast the beet in the oven for 45 minutes. Remove and let cool. You can speed up the cooling process by putting the cooked beet in the refrigerator or freezer for a few minutes. Cutting it also helps it cool faster.

In a high-speed blender, combine the cooled roasted beet, strawberry jam, coconut sugar, almond milk, olive oil, and vanilla. Blend until smooth. Pour the mixture into a large bowl.

In a small bowl, mix the almond flour, coconut flour, and sea salt. Stir the dry ingredients into the wet ingredients. Fold in the chocolate chips. Stir until completely mixed.

Refrigerate the dough for 30 minutes. Roll the chilled dough into 1½-inch (3.5 cm) balls. Store any leftover dough balls in the freezer for up to 1 month.

YIELD: 36 BALLS

✳ BEET LOVE

I love beets because they're packed full of vitamins and nutrients like folate, manganese, and potassium; they aren't expensive; they're one of the sweetest vegetables; and they're super versatile! Plus, they're a beautiful color.

Sweet Potato Brownies

This is our go-to fudgy brownie recipe. And I absolutely love that these brownies have more veggies than flour!

Cooking spray

½ *of a sweet potato*

⅔ *cup (75 g) coconut flour*

⅔ *cup (57 g) cocoa powder*

½ *cup (72 g) coconut sugar*

1 *teaspoon baking powder*

2 *cups (60 g) fresh baby spinach*

½ *cup (120 ml) chocolate almond milk*

¼ *cup (60 ml) extra-virgin olive oil*

3 *eggs*

½ *cup (88 g) mini chocolate chips*

Powdered sugar, for dusting (optional)

Preheat the oven to 350°F (180°C, or gas mark 4). Spray a 9 x 9-inch (23 x23 cm) baking dish with nonstick cooking spray and set aside.

Microwave the sweet potato for 4 minutes on high and then carefully peel off the skin.

In a small bowl, combine the coconut flour, cocoa powder, coconut sugar, and baking powder. Stir until thoroughly mixed. Set aside.

In a high-speed blender, combine the sweet potato, spinach, chocolate almond milk, and olive oil. Blend until smooth. Pour the purée into a large bowl and then whisk in the eggs.

Slowly stir the flour mixture into the sweet potato purée, adding about one-third at a time, stirring well to combine. Fold in the chocolate chips. Pour the brownie batter into the prepared dish. Bake for 25 minutes.

Serve warm or cold. They're great with a sprinkle of powdered sugar on top (if using).

YIELD: 9 TO 12 BROWNIES

✴ COCONUT FLOUR'S MAGIC

One of the things I love about using coconut flour is that it is super absorbent, so you can use a lot of wet ingredients, such as in this recipe: ½ cup (120 ml) chocolate almond milk, olive oil, plus puréed veggies, and 3 eggs!

Super-Creamy Chocolate Pudding Pops

You've probably seen some recipes floating around the Internet for a chocolate-avocado pudding made with avocados and cocoa powder. I've tried a few and haven't really liked any of them. These pudding pops are different. Perfectly creamy and chocolatey and sweet, you will be making these all summer long!

1 avocado

2 cups (475 ml) chocolate almond milk

½ cup (43 g) cocoa powder

¼ cup (80 g) dark amber maple syrup

1 teaspoon vanilla extract

Pinch of sea salt

In a high-speed blender, combine the avocado, chocolate almond milk, cocoa powder, maple syrup, vanilla, and sea salt. Blend until smooth.

Pour the chocolate mixture into an ice pop mold. Freeze for 3 to 4 hours before serving.

YIELD: 10 POPS

Strawberry Ombre Pops

Let's just agree now, these are the cutest ice pops ever! They are bright, vivid, and bold, colored completely naturally from real fruit and veggies frozen in separate layers. Don't let the cuteness fool you, though; they pack a nutritional punch that your kids will beg to eat!

FOR ROASTED BEET:

½ of a beet, peeled

1 teaspoon extra-virgin olive oil

FOR POPS:

⅔ cup (154 g) strawberry Greek yogurt

½ cup (120 ml) unsweetened almond milk

1 small banana

1 teaspoon vanilla extract

¾ cup (175 ml) acai berry juice

¼ cup (48 g) raw cane sugar

6 fresh strawberries

¼ cup (80 g) organic strawberry jam

TO ROAST THE BEET: Preheat the oven to 425°F (220°C, or gas mark 7). Place the beet on aluminum foil, brush with olive oil, and then fold the foil around the beet so it is covered. Bake for 45 minutes and then cool in the fridge before continuing.

TO MAKE THE POPS: In a high-speed blender, combine the strawberry Greek yogurt, almond milk, banana, and vanilla. Blend until smooth. Pour this mixture into a 10-pop ice pop mold, filling each mold one-third full. Freeze the pops for 1 hour. There will be a little mixture leftover; that's good.

To the leftover mixture in the blender, add the acai berry juice, sugar, and strawberries. Blend until smooth and refrigerate as the first layer freezes.

Once the first layer is thoroughly frozen, pour the strawberry layer into the molds. Each pop will now be about two-thirds full. Freeze the pops for 1 hour more. There will be a little mixture leftover; that's good.

To the leftover mixture in the blender, add the roasted beet and strawberry jam. Blend until smooth and refrigerate as the second layer freezes.

Once the second layer is thoroughly frozen, pour the beet layer on top, filling each mold completely. Freeze the pops for 2 hours more before serving.

YIELD: 10 POPS

✳ NO TIME FOR OMBRE?

If you don't need or want the layering effect or just want to save time, blend all the ingredients together at the start! The pops taste fantastic this way, too.

Sweet Potato Dessert Nachos

Oh my goodness gracious, you need these in your life! Sweet potato chips are topped with an almond butter–coffee drizzle, perfectly toasted marshmallows, melted chocolate chips, and shredded coconut. Did I mention they're delicious?

FOR SAUCE:

2 tablespoons (32 g) almond butter

2 tablespoons (28 ml) brewed coffee, cooled

½ teaspoon coconut sugar

½ teaspoon ground cinnamon

FOR NACHOS:

1 bag (6 ounces, or 170 g) sweet potato chips

¼ cup (44 g) mini dark chocolate chips

¼ cup (25 g) mini marshmallows

¼ cup (15 g) unsweetened coconut flakes

Preheat the oven to 375°F (190°C, or gas mark 5). Line a baking sheet with parchment paper and set aside.

TO MAKE THE SAUCE: In a small bowl, mix the almond butter, coffee, coconut sugar, and cinnamon. Microwave for 30 seconds on high and then stir so the ingredients are completely melted and combined.

TO MAKE THE NACHOS: Spread half of the sweet potato chips in a single layer onto the prepared sheet. Sprinkle the chips with half each of the chocolate chips, mini marshmallows, and coconut.

Drizzle on half of the sauce.

Place another layer of the remaining sweet potato chips on top. Sprinkle with the remaining chocolate chips, mini marshmallows, coconut, and sauce.

Bake for 5 to 8 minutes until the marshmallows are softened and lightly browned and the chocolate is melted. Serve with napkins at the ready.

YIELD: 4 SERVINGS

Peach Cobbler with Quinoa

Sweet, soft, sugary peaches are intermingled with a cake-like cobbler and topped with vanilla ice cream in this delicious summery dessert!

Cooking spray

FOR PEACHES:

6 fresh peaches, pitted and sliced
or frozen and thawed

¼ cup (36 g) coconut sugar

¼ cup (60 ml) water

1 tablespoon (8 g) cornstarch

¼ teaspoon ground cinnamon

FOR COBBLER:

¾ cup (94 g) white whole-wheat
flour

1½ teaspoons baking powder

1 cup (191 g) Quinoa-Lentil Blend
(page 18)

½ cup (120 ml) unsweetened
almond milk

⅓ cup (80 ml) extra-virgin
olive oil

2 tablespoons (40 g) dark amber
maple syrup

2 tablespoons (18 g) coconut sugar

½ teaspoon sea salt

1 ½ cups (210 g) vanilla ice cream

Preheat the oven to 400°F (200°C, or gas mark 6). Spray a 9 x 9-inch (23 x 23 cm) baking dish with nonstick cooking spray and set aside.

TO MAKE THE PEACHES: In a medium saucepan over medium heat, combine the sliced peaches, coconut sugar, and water. Simmer for about 8 minutes and then stir in the cornstarch and cinnamon to thicken the mixture. Pour the peaches into the prepared dish and set aside.

TO MAKE THE COBBLER: In a small bowl, mix the flour and baking powder.

In a large bowl, stir together the Quinoa-Lentil Blend, almond milk, olive oil, maple syrup, coconut sugar, and sea salt until thoroughly combined.

Slowly stir the flour mixture into the wet ingredients. Place large dollops of the dough on top of the peaches.

Bake for 45 minutes or until the cobbler is lightly browned on top. Serve hot with vanilla ice cream.

YIELD: 6 SERVINGS

✳ SUMMER BERRY VERSION

I love substituting fresh blueberries, blackberries, and strawberries for the peaches to make a berry cobbler version in summer when organic berries are so plentiful and inexpensive!

Easy Olive Oil Cake

This easy olive oil cake is everything: rich, flavorful, decadent, airy, and light with a crispy edge, completely gluten-free (though you'd never guess it!), and perfectly sweet and delish. It is my go-to dessert for all parties and get-togethers.

Olive oil cooking spray

**FOR CAKE:**

2 cups (272 g) gluten-free all-purpose baking flour or (250 g) white whole-wheat flour

2 teaspoons (9 g) baking powder

½ teaspoon sea salt

1 ripe banana

¾ cup (175 ml) extra virgin olive oil

½ cup (120 ml) unsweetened almond milk

1 teaspoon vanilla extract

3 eggs

¾ cup (108 g) coconut sugar

FOR TOPPING:

¾ cup (131 g) dark chocolate chips (62 percent cacao or higher is recommended)

3 tablespoons (45 ml) chocolate almond milk

1½ teaspoons coconut oil

¼ cup (30 g) chopped walnuts

Preheat oven to 350°F (180°C, or gas mark 4). Spray a bundt pan with the olive oil cooking spray and set aside.

TO MAKE THE CAKE: In a large mixing bowl, combine the flour, baking powder, and sea salt. Stir to combine and set aside.

In a small mixing bowl, mash the banana. Stir in the olive oil, almond milk, and vanilla. Set aside.

In another small bowl, combine the eggs and coconut sugar. Using a hand mixer, mix for 2 to 3 minutes on medium-high speed. Then, pour the egg mixture into the banana mixture and stir thoroughly to combine.

Add the wet ingredients to the dry ingredients and stir until just combined. Do not overmix. Pour the batter into the prepared bundt pan and bake for 45 minutes until the cake is nicely golden brown and a knife inserted comes out clean. Remove from the oven and let cool on the counter for at least 15 minutes. Flip the pan onto a parchment paper–lined cake plate.

TO MAKE THE TOPPING: In a small saucepan over low heat, combine the chocolate chips, chocolate almond milk, and coconut oil. Stir continually until melted.

Drizzle the melted chocolate over the cooled cake. Then, sprinkle with the walnuts.

Use a cake spatula to lift the cake and remove the parchment. (You can skip the parchment layer, if you don't mind some chocolate drizzle on your cake plate!)

YIELD: 8 SERVINGS

Recipe Notes

List your favorites, your changes, and what you'd like to make next!

Share the Love!

Please share any photos of the recipes you make with #superfoodweeknights to Instagram: @noshandnourish and Facebook: @noshandnourish.

PICTURED: SPINACH PESTO PIZZA FROM PAGE 79.

Acknowledgments

To Amanda and Winnie, my editors, thank you for believing in this book from the beginning, and, more than that, for your commitment to me—as a writer and as a photographer. We have created (*another*) something truly beautiful together!

To Mary, my copyeditor, and Marissa, my art director, thank you for your attention to every detail and your commitment to make this book the absolute best it could be.

To Danny, thank you for your intense pickiness about food. You helped make this book better, tasting and providing feedback on every recipe and guaranteeing that if you liked it, almost anyone would. There were some intense weeks, with probably more quinoa and avocado than you would prefer to eat at one time, and yet you supported me gracefully. Thank you for your willingness to incorporate more superfoods into your diet and to eat more (*delicious*) vegetarian meals, all in the name of health.

To Babycakes, thank you for helping me design and color the front of this cookbook and taste test every single recipe! You are the reason I started thinking about food differently and why I fell in love with cooking. Thank you for challenging me daily to love Jesus more, to be compassionate toward others, and to focus on the things that really matter. You have a fire burning inside that I did not create, and I want to fan the flame, not extinguish it. I really can't say I love you enough—I love you. I love you. I LOVE YOU!!! I want constantly to smother your neck with kisses, sing you a thousand "twinkle twinkles," laugh until our bellies hurt, and celebrate who you become. You make my heart full.

To Mom, thank you for being my biggest cheerleader! Thanks for truly caring about every detail in this book as much as I do. I couldn't have done it without you. I can't wait to have you living close by so we can enjoy these recipes together, over a glass of wine (*or two*)!

To Dad, thank you for instilling in me a genuine passion and enthusiasm for good food, for teaching me the sky's the limit, for equipping me with the "WIN—what's important now" strategy so I could juggle writing a (*second*) book, raising a vibrant little girl, and working part time successfully. Last but not least, thank you for telling me daily how proud you are of me. It means the world to me.

To Shawna, God put you in my life at just the right time! A friend who is totally obsessed with cookbooks, adores cooking, and truly celebrates and loves talking about all things food. I couldn't have done it without you. Thank you for your support, encouragement, and overall enthusiasm for this project.

To my *Nosh and Nourish* blog readers and taste testers, please accept my utmost thanks for the support, enthusiasm, and excitement you've given me over the past four years. Thank you for your honest feedback, your thousand "thank yous" and "*OMG . . . so good*"s, your enthusiasm for what's next, and your habit of reading my blog day after day. To know my recipes help you live happier, healthier lives means the world to me. You are why I am here today, finishing the acknowledgments for my second cookbook! I can't wait for it to be in your hands and in your kitchens!

About the Author

For the first 30 years of her life, Kelly Pfeiffer didn't enjoy, er . . . *hated* cooking. She often found herself in the kitchen mid-cooking realizing she was missing an important ingredient—like when making Honey Dijon Chicken and discovering she didn't have any mustard! The shift came when she realized she much preferred looking into the pantry, seeing what was on hand, and creating something from scratch rather than trying to follow someone else's recipe. And, in doing so, she discovered she was quite talented at creating delicious, unique, and nourishing recipes—and that she actually enjoyed it!

In March 2012, Kelly started the blog *Nosh and Nourish* to showcase her recipes and exquisite food photography and inspire others to live a happy, healthy life. Her goal is to make healthy eating seem doable in the hustle and bustle of everyday life. She is the author of the cookbook, *Superfoods at Every Meal*—that has had great success and is printed in over six languages! Her food and recipes have been featured in *Women's Fitness* magazine, *Fox News Magazine*, *Cosmopolitan*, *Elle*, *Country Living*, *Parade* magazine, and *The Huffington Post*. When not creating new recipes or taking pictures of them, she can be found exploring the mountains, gardening, hiking, or fly-fishing. She and her husband live with their daughter and two beagles in a small mountain town outside of Denver, Colorado. Kelly's blog can be found online at: www.noshandnourish.com.

Index